PENGUIN
ARKANA

FENG SHUI

Sarah Rossbach lived, worked, and studied in Asia for two years. She was graduated from Barnard College and Columbia University Graduate School of Journalism where she received the Far East Asian Journalism Fellowship. Her articles have appeared in the *New York Times*, the *Asian Wall Street Journal, Travel and Leisure* and *Art & Auction*. She now lives in the New York City area. Her desk and bed are in lucky positions.

The characters representing feng shui.

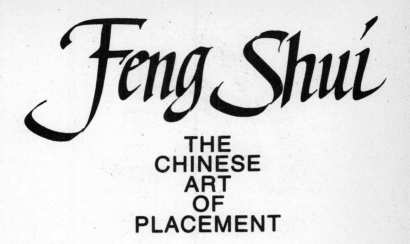

Feng Shui

THE CHINESE ART OF PLACEMENT

Sarah Rossbach

ARKANA

ARKANA
Published by the Penguin Group
Penguin Books USA Inc.,
375 Hudson Street, New York, New York 10014, U.S.A
Penguin Books Ltd, 27 Wrights Lane,
London W8 5TZ, England
Penguin Books Australia Ltd, Ringwood,
Victoria, Australia
Penguin Books Canada Ltd, 10 Alcorn Avenue,
Toronto, Ontario, Canada M4V 3B2
Penguin Books (N.Z.) Ltd, 182–190 Wairau Road,
Auckland 10, New Zealand

Penguin Books Ltd, Registered Offices:
Harmondsworth, Middlesex, England

First published in the United States of America by E. P. Dutton
Published simultaneously in Canada by Fitzhenry & Whiteside, Limited, Toronto
Published in Arkana Books 1991

13   15   17   19   20   18   16   14   12

ISBN 0 14 019.353 7

Printed in the United States of America
Calligraphy by Lin Yun
Illustrations by David Acheson

To those who were in the right place at the right time.

CONTENTS

CONTENTS

PREFACE

In 1977, while living and working in Hong Kong, I began Chinese lessons with a man named Lin Yun. Vague stories circulated around the colony of his prowess in an ancient art called *feng shui*. I knew that feng shui translated literally is "wind" and "water," but beyond that I had only a sketchy idea that it had something to do with the ambience of a place. Lin Yun and I would begin our classes in the opulent, colonial-style lobby of the Peninsula Hotel, sipping orange juice and talking of the heroic exploits of Chairman Mao, but more often than not, our dialogues would get short shrift. A young bellhop would circulate through the massive lobby ringing a bell and parading a sign paging Lin Yun. On returning to the table, Professor Lin would say, "Don't pay me for this lesson. I have to look at a friend's mother's grave. Would you join me?"

So I'd shut my textbook and off we'd go on his feng shui rounds: the home of an American journalist whose marriage was rocky, the grave of the mother of an investment banker whose holdings were shaky, the office of a jeweler whose store had been robbed, even the home of a doctor who suffered from insomnia and migraines.

During those lessons, I gradually began to understand what this mysterious "feng shui" actually means. I saw that it combines mystical meaning, common sense, and, sometimes, good taste. I learned that it could involve everything from chairs to corners, from architecture to astrology—determining dates for weddings, festivals, funerals, parties, and even mundane chores such as chopping trees and mowing lawns. But it is more than that. It is an eco-art dealing with conservation, ecology, orientation, and spatial arrange-ment—basically how and where man should place himself or build his shelter in this vast world. It is a means to define one's position in the physical universe, and then improve on it. And I discovered that it held the promise of everything anyone could possibly want: happy family, good marriage, healthy and long life, successful career, wealth, good luck....In its full scope, feng shui tells us how to locate ourselves in the universe in a better way.

Most of the inspiration for this book belongs to Lin Yun. Though each feng shui practitioner has a different approach, good feng shui demands he act as philosopher, psychologist, doctor, father confessor, and interior designer all rolled into one. Lin Yun is one of the foremost living adepts of this complex art.

A Mandarin teacher by day and a feng shui man by night, Lin Yun began his training when he was six years old. Born in Peking in 1932, he used to play with friends on the grounds of a Tibetan Bud-dhist temple near his family's home. The temple housed several lamas trained in the Tantric Black Hat sect, a mystical sect of Tibetan Buddhism. One day, a monk approached the boys and offered them lessons in religion. While Lin Yun's friends ran away, he ventured closer to hear what the monk had to say. For the next nine years, Lin Yun was instructed in the writings and practices of the sect. These included both Tibetan Tantric mystical arts and traditional Chinese texts and teachings, such as the *I Ching* and feng shui. Since then, he has studied law, philosophy, and urban planning, and has lectured on feng shui in the United States.

The early chapters of this book give an overview of feng shui tradition, history, and method shared by all experts, and the later chapters are generally based on Lin Yun's treatment of feng shui—his practice, teachings, and experience.

I found feng shui appealing, though, frankly, I was skeptical at first. I don't know why or how it operates—I'm not a scientist—but I do know it has worked for many people for thousands of years. And, in the five years of studying it, I've seen marriages saved, careers made, and restaurants prosper. You may call it coincidence, but I can testify that it works.

I should like to thank the following people who were generous with their time, knowledge, and hospitality: Vivien Chang, Tong Yi-fang, Suzanne Green, Lynne Curry, Lucy Lo, Sylvia Edgar, Eric Cumine, Tao Ho, David Lung, Di-mon Lu, Veronica Hwang Li, Doris Wang, Mrs. Margery Topley, Mike Chinoy, Shao Fon-fon, John Warden, James Hayes, Robert Upton, John Chu, Barbara Butterfield, Rockwell Stensrud, Ching Cruz, George Lee, Dr. William Whitson, David Keh, Johnny Kao, George Hsu, The Hong Kong Tourist Association, the Ossabaw Island Project, Georgia, Ju Mu, Christine Douglas, Ernie Munch, Penny Coleman, two Hong Kong feng shui experts, Choi Pak-lai and Chen To-Sang; and a Singapore feng shui adept and exhumer, Tan Chat Lung.

PREFACE

I should also like to express special thanks to Spencer Reiss for reading this manuscript in all its incarnations, to David Acheson for his architectural comments and drawings, to Glenn Cowley for his advice and encouragement, and to the late June Shaplen for her support in all stages of this book. Most important, I am especially grateful to Lin Yun for his time, knowledge, and patience with this project, and without whom it would never have been written.

SARAH ROSSBACH

New York 1983

CHRONOLOGY

Shang	c. 1766–c. 1123 B.C.
Chou	c. 1122–256
Ch'in	221–207
Han	202 B.C.–A.D. 221
Six dynasties	221–581
Sui	581–618
T'ang	618–906
Five dynasties	907–960

CHRONOLOGY

Sung	960–1279
Yüan (Mongols)	1260–1368
Ming	1368–1644
Ch'ing (Manchus)	1644–1912
Republic	1912–
People's Republic	1949–

GLOSSARY

amah   A Chinese nurse or servant.

ba-gua   An eight-sided symbol of the *I Ching*, with eight
   trigrams.

ch'i   Cosmic breath, human energy.

chung-guo   "The Middle Kingdom," China.

chu-shr   That which is outside our realm of experience, that is,
   illogical cures.

feng shui   "Wind" and "water," the Chinese art of placement.

jusha   A red, non-edible, medicinal/mystical powder.

karma   The Buddhist concept which holds that one's destiny is determined by one's own good and bad deeds, performed in this and past lives.

li   A Chinese mile.

ling   Airborne particles of embryonic human ch'i.

lo   Cantonese for "priest."

ru-shr   That which is within our realm of experience, that is, logical cures.

Tao, Taoism   "The Way," a philosophical concept of unity. A religion and philosophy deriving from this concept.

tsai   "Food" and "money."

Tun Fu ceremony   A spirit-placating rite.

tzu wei   The North Star.

yin-yang theory   The Taoist concept that unifies all opposites.

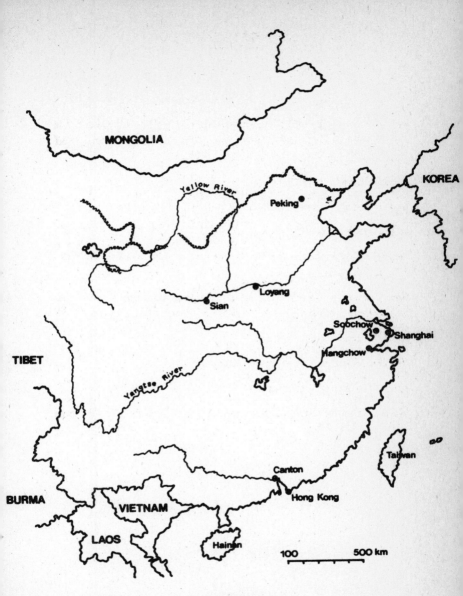

Map of China.

Feng Shui

One

INTRODUCTION: EXPLAINING FENG SHUI

The Chinese often trace success or failure not so much to human actions, but to the workings of mysterious earth forces. Known as *feng shui*—literally "wind" and "water"—these forces are believed to be responsible for determining health, prosperity, and good luck. Ancient Chinese emperors consulted feng shui experts before building huge public works or waging war. Chiang Kai-shek's rise to power is traced to the especiallly good feng shui of his mother's grave; his downfall is blamed on the Communists later digging it up. Some say kung-fu king Bruce Lee's untimely demise occured because he lived in an unlucky house.

Though officially suppressed in the People's Republic of China, feng shui is today still widely but surreptitiously practiced, mostly in the countryside. It flourishes in Hong Kong, where it is also often used in one form or another by most Chinese and even some Westerners. It has begun to spread to the United States. One Hong Kong and Shanghai Bank officer said, "If my clients believe it, well, so do I."

For all the mystery that surrounds it, feng shui evolved from the simple observation that people are affected, for good or ill, by surroundings: the layout and orientation of workplaces and homes. In addition, the Chinese have long observed that some surroundings are better, luckier, or more blessed than others. Every hill, building, wall, window, and corner and the ways in which they face wind and water have an effect. They concluded that if you change surroundings, you can change your life. The aim of feng shui, then, is to change and harmonize the environment—cosmic currents known as *ch'i*—to improve fortunes.

Feng shui has broadly been applied from the smallest of spaces—say, a bedroom or even the location of a chair—to the largest, cosmic dimension. Its philosophical roots span a whole range of Chinese thought from Taoism and Buddhism to rural magic. It operates on many levels: superstitious and practical, sacred and profane, emotional and physical. There are even those who draw parallels to Western psychology and scientific thought, and believe that its metaphysics operates similarly to modern physics, linking all matter and all mind in one unified theory. Carl Jung wrote, 'The ancient Chinese mind contemplates the cosmos in a way comparable to that of the modern physicist, who cannot deny that his model of the world is a decidedly psychophysical structure.''*

In practice, feng shui is something between a science and an

---

*Carl Jung, Foreword to *The I Ching or Book of Changes*, trans. Richard Wilhelm (Princeton, N.J.: Princeton University Press, 1950), p. xxiv.

art. Westerners often call it *geomancy*[*] but the two are not really identical. Feng shui encompasses more than geomancy. Besides arranging living quarters with optimal comfort for mind and body, feng shui also includes astrological and other "psychic" aspects. Experts consider orientation (often with the aid of a cosmic compass), configurations, and juxtapositions. Lin Yun, a leading Hong Kong feng shui expert, explains, "I adapt homes to harmonize with the currents of ch'i," meaning man's nature and cosmic breath. "The shapes of beds, the forms and heights of buildings, and the directions of roads and corners all modify a person's destiny." With that in mind, an international design competition for a multimillion-dollar complex in Hong Kong stressed, along with the usual technical stipulations, feng shui as a crucial consideration.

Fees for feng shui advice vary widely. Choi Pak-lai, one of Hong Kong's most famous feng shui priests, commands roughly sixty cents a square foot for a consultation. Shau Fon-fon, who attended college in the United States, but is now an actress and businesswoman in Hong Kong, moved into a new, spacious apartment and spent $10,000 on interior design—$3,000 of it related to feng shui.

Feng shui is so extensive in Hong Kong that people joke that the practitioner must be in cahoots with building contractors or at least hold stock in a mirror factory (mirrors figure prominently as feng shui cures). Even the commodities exchange is not immune. A commodities reporter noted the marked improvement on the cotton exchange after its exit was changed from a simple door opening onto a small lobby to a revolving one leading to a spacious loading platform.

Although few feng shui practitioners in Hong Kong speak

----

[*] *The Oxford English Dictionary* definition is "The art of divination by means of signs derived from the earth, as by the figure assumed by a handful of earth thrown down upon some surface—hence, usually, divination by means of lines or figures formed by jotting down on paper a number of dots at random."

English, the American Chamber of Commerce, the *Far Eastern Economic Review*, and N. M. Rothschild, the British merchant bank, have all used feng shui services. Ignatius Lau, a Hong Kong architect, says that before any offical building is constructed the British colonial government consults with local feng shui priests to see if the structures are ritually aligned with wind and water. Even *Newsweek*'s executive editor, Maynard Parker, says that though he didn't take much stock in feng shui, when he was warned that a Hong Kong apartment he was considering renting had bad feng shui, he searched elsewhere for suitable living quarters.

Feng shui has migrated to the United States. A New York woman, after living in a luxury apartment for ten years, happened to consult a feng shui man. The prognosis wasn't good. She must move, he said, if she was to survive. Within a week of the visit she did—and as far as I know she is still alive. Graphic artist Milton Glaser's office had been robbed six times, so he sent the layout and seating plan to a Hong Kong expert. Since he followed instructions—installing a tank with six black fish and hanging a red clock—the office has been secure. In Washington, D.C., in 1980, before Johnny Kau opened his restaurant House of Hunan on a site where two previous businesses had failed, he sought feng shui advice on his $800,000 worth of renovations. Today, he says, business is booming as a result of feng shui. "Things took off more than I expected," he comments, looking around at full tables and a long waiting line.

Despite its pragmatic aspect, feng shui is in a sense a rosetta stone linking man and his environment, ancient ways and modern life. It interprets the language articulated by natural forms and phenomena, by man-made buildings and symbols, and by the continual workings of the universe, including moon phases and star alignments. Feng shui is the key to understanding the silent dialogue between man and nature, whispered through a cosmic breath or spirit—ch'i. The Chinese term *ch'i* is a life force or energy that ripples water, creates mountains, breathes life into plants, trees, and humans, and propels man along a life course. If ch'i is misguided, man's life and luck might falter. Man feels and is affected by ch'i, though he may not know it.

Feng shui experts fill the need to intuit, decode, and interpret our environment. They watch for patterns in nature and for the human reaction to it. They listen to the symphony of interrelated occurrences and to the unseen cosmic powers governing the universe and affecting our bodies, minds, and, ultimately, our fates.

Two

ORIGINS

I climb the road to Cold Mountain,
the road to Cold Mountain that never ends.
The valleys are long and strewn with boulders,
the streams broad and banked with thick grass.
Moss is slippery though no rain has fallen;
pines sigh but it isn't wind.
Who can break from the snares of the world
and sit with me among the white clouds? . . .

Among a thousand clouds and ten thousand streams
here lives an idle man,
in the daytime wandering over green mountains,
at night coming home to sleep by the cliff.
Swiftly the springs and autumns pass,
but my mind is at peace, free of dust and delusion.
How pleasant, to know I need nothing to lean on,
to be still as the waters of the autumn river!

—Han-Shan, "Cold Mountain"*

China has no shortage of awesome landscapes. For centuries the Chinese have drawn inspiration from snaking, craggy mountain ranges with peaks melting into misty sky to rivers weaving through fertile valleys and feeding a patchwork of yellow and green oddly shaped rice paddies. Eighth-century poets celebrated nature in verse, courting the moon, sky, mountains, and streams. T'ang dynasty (A.D. 618–906) painters glorified nature's vastness, power, and peace: on silk scrolls, they created miniature panoramas of jagged, towering peaks, razor-straight waterfalls cascading through clouds into terraces and gorges, tiny footbridges crossed by even smaller hermit sages. Taoist thinkers became disciples of nature: idealizing it, seeking a harmony with the natural "way," an identity with the cosmos. Poets, artists, and philosophers alike all yearned to fit into the grand scheme, the harmony and immortality of nature. From this reverence for nature sprang early Chinese religion (Taoism), science (astronomy, geology, magnetism, and alchemy), superstition (astrology, shamanism, fortune-telling), and lastly—a peculiar combination of all three—feng shui.

*Han-Shan, *Cold Mountain: 100 Poems by Han-Shan,* trans. Burton Watson (New York: Grove Press, 1962), pp. 58, 79.

MAN AND NATURE (Chinese-Style)

The Chinese saw a magical link between man and the landscape: Nature reacts to any change and that reaction resounds in man. They saw the world and themselves as part of a sacred metabolic system. Everything pulsed with life. Everything depended on everything else. The Chinese felt they shared a fate with the earth: When it was healthy and prospered, they thrived; when the balance was destroyed, they suffered. So it made sense, in feng shui terms, to enhance the environment rather than to harm or deplete it, thus hurting the chances for good luck and happiness.

The roots of feng shui grow out of a primitive agrarian way of life, when the fate of man was inextricably bound up with the whims and cycles of heaven and earth: with weather, fertility of the earth, floods, accessibility of water, and amount of sunlight. Man was vulnerable to nature, so he kept watch on it.

From the semidivine emperor—the go-between of heaven and earth—to the laboring peasant, a yearly concern was successful crops. Both ruler and subject looked to nature for signs of drought, flood, and famine. In agriculture, the farmer depended on nature for his life source. In government, the emperor looked to nature for reaffirmation of his right to rule, the mandate of heaven. Since the Chou dynasty (1122–256 B.C.), emperors made annual appeals to heaven on behalf of their kingdom for good crops, good health, and peace. A natural disaster signified that an emperor had lost the balance between heaven and earth, leaving him vulnerable to overthrow. So he relied on special advisers to look for and to interpret omens.

Control of nature's creative and destructive forces—harnessing wind and channeling water—was therefore crucial. "He who controls water, governs the empire,"* is an old Chinese saying. An

*Paul Sun, trans., "Feng Shui: An Ancient Theory of Village Siting," in *The Village as Solar Ecology* (East Falmouth, Mass.: The New Alchemy Institute, 1980), p. 22.

emperor's hold on power depended on controlling both floods, rivers, and canals.

In China—a nation slightly larger than the United States, including Alaska—natural conditions vary widely. In north China, where cold winds rip through houses, mountains and trees provide screens. In the south, where floods annually threaten crops, homes, and lives, mountains provide elevation and irrigation lessens damage. In flat, loessial soil regions, such as the Loyang area, where winds whip up sands, the Chinese dug a network of tunnel homes as shelter from the wind.

Thousands of years ago, as Chinese civilization sprang up along the fertile Yellow and Wei river valleys, feng shui's basic premises also developed from the topographical and geographical nature of the area, a mixture of rugged mountains, plateaus, rivers, valleys, and plains. Long before there were architects, natural phenomena such as wind and water were viewed as sacred signs mysteriously instructing shamans where the most auspicious place was for a house, an altar, or a grave.

The ancient Chinese found that a house sited halfway up a hill on the north side of the river facing south received optimal sun, was protected from harsh winds, avoided floods, and still had access to water for crops. In such surroundings, it was easiest to survive: rice, vegetables, and fruit-bearing trees grew under an unhindered sun, cattle grazed on lush grass, and a house stayed relatively warm in the winter. The environment proved comfortable and harmonious, and helped inhabitants to survive and to grow successful and even wealthy.

When that significant, auspicious, and ideal space was unattainable, the search for antidotes led to the study of feng shui. Soon thereafter, the pursuit and fabrication of a viable physical setting became a basic environmental science, with its goal the control of man's immediate surroundings.

Feng shui supports the modern idea of ecology and conservation. Its message is: Harmonize with, do not disrupt, nature.

Tampering with nature might disrupt its equilibrium. Costs of changing the environment range from pollution to overpopulation. Changes must therefore be planned and executed carefully. Indiscriminate altering of nature can set off a series of events leading to unpredictable results. (The Chinese did not always practice what they preached. Throughout the nineteenth and twentieth centuries, they lumbered extensively in the north for firewood and consequently drastically altered the ecological balance, changing dense forest into a dust bowl.)

THE SACRED ART OF POSITIONING

The Chinese have always stressed position, be it within the landscape, the world, or the cosmos. And to locate the correct spot, they used mystical methods ranging from numerology and astrology to orientation and images. For example, they sought meaning through designating cities, buildings, and people with names implying and invoking central power. China itself, *Chung-guo,* means "Middle Kingdom"—the nation at the hub of the universe, the heart to which all power flows and from which even greater power emanates. In Peking, the emperor's domain, the "Purple Forbidden City," (*Tzu Chin Ch'eng*), alludes to the North Star, *Tzu Wei,* the constellation around which all stars revolve. There the emperor, the son of heaven, mediated the country's fate, keeping peace between heaven, earth, and man.

But power and good fortune came initially from the landscape. The Chinese invested their surroundings with sacred meanings derived from natural shapes, growth, and orientation. The earth had many guises ranging from dragon to disembodied god, all possessing a cosmic power that ruled man's destiny. The entire Chinese universe was imbued with sacred gods, spirits, and creatures, who lived in heaven and earth, moon and sun, sea and land.

The Chinese cosmos, however, was holistic, tying all natural features into one body. In one creation myth, the landscape itself was not just a chaotic and hostile mass of mountains, rivers, and forest, but a god figure transformed.

> The origin of the world lay in a primordial egg which hatched a god who lived 18,000 years. Then he died. His head split and became the sun and moon, his blood the rivers and seas, his hair the plants, his limbs the mountains, his voice the thunder, his perspiration the rain, his breath the wind—and his fleas the ancestors of man.*

So the Chinese were building not on an undefined, unknown wilderness but on the flesh of a god figure, who once had human form and spawned and fed human parasites. On a religious level, feng shui is an attempt to communicate with and to attain blessings and power from the primordial god/earth, tapping its resources and power.

FENG SHUI EXPERTS

Feng shui experts are at once the priests and the doctors of environmental ills. They hold the sacred and profane knowledge of the fates of man and earth. As priests, they read and interpret both visible and invisible signs and positive forces in the cosmos. They define man's place in the universe. As doctors, they detect the earth's pulse, determining where man will live the most healthy, productive, prosperous, and happy life, and where buildings will least disturb the earth's circulation.

Being receptive to the environment, the feng shui expert can analyze physical settings such as mountains, trees, wind, water, and

---

*Maggie Keswick, *The Chinese Garden* (New York: Rizzoli, 1978), p. 29.

star alignments. Most likely, the early feng shui man was similar to a rainmaker. He gathered information from his surroundings, reading signs and forewarnings in breezes, leaf colors, moon rings, the smell of rain, insect and animal behavior, rock moisture, and stars. To stay in step with nature's best ch'i and to gain power from it requires special talents and special knowledge. As Lin Yun explains:

> We possess many senses, not just the five common senses—hearing, smelling, tasting, seeing and touching—but many more. We all have insights. We pick up feelings from people, places, dreams, atmospheric energy. Some people give us a sense of foreboding. Some places make us feel happy and comfortable. We pick up these yet-to-be-named feelings and intuit reality and destiny from that.

He claims people possess more than one hundred "senses," most of which are latent. Feng shui experts have developed their senses to be more keenly aware, more tuned into the environment—like a shortwave radio, they use psychic antennae to pick up messages, signals, and static from their surroundings.

Today feng shui is a complex system that some Chinese choose to handle themselves, while most call for professional advice. Advice varies because of the different theories practiced today. Around the third century A.D., feng shui divided into two principal schools. One, developed in Fukien province, stressed direction and depended on a cosmic compass, where the relationship of various elements in the Chinese universe—the stars, the *I Ching or Book of Changes,* and others—are charted in concentric circles around a compass. The other, originating in Kiangsi province, was concerned with shapes and directions of land and water masses. In the twelfth century, feng shui blossomed through the metaphysical theories of Chu Hsi, a respected scholar who stressed the "investigation of things (leading to) the extension of knowledge."

Historically, feng shui men ranged from semiliterates and

scholars to Buddhist and Taoist priests. Though there are several feng shui texts, much of the information has been passed down orally, often from father to son. (A feng shui woman did not exist, because Confucian custom prevented transmitting important and sacred knowledge to females: "Teach sons, not daughters.")

In the Chinese eye, feng shui experts, as in most vocations, run the gamut from wise man to charlatan. Some hold positions of respect in communities and use feng shui not only to divine sites, but also to settle local disputes. Others, however, are less public minded, milking residents of money and giving feng shui rhetoric in return. At the turn of the century, near Canton, for example, one geomancer charged a whopping $3,000 for choosing an auspicious burial site for a wealthy woman. Feng shui frauds are not infrequent: They assign bogus cures, leading some skeptics to use "feng shui professor" as another term for liar.

The Chinese are not beyond invoking the mystical to solve the mundane. While a few with a philosophical bent might see feng shui as a way to stay in step with the cosmos, the more ambitious see it as a necessary edge over others in life. Still, many view feng shui as a paradox: While some scorn it as superstition, most don't turn their backs on it completely, suspecting that feng shui experts possess an innate special wisdom, power, and knowledge.

Feng shui experts guard the secrets of their practice. This practice crops up in various incarnations in Korea, Japan, Laos, Thailand, the Philippines, Vietnam, Malaysia, and Singapore. Feng shui methods are tailored to a range of local needs; a village wise man in Malacca, Malaysia; a graveside exhumer in rapidly developing Singapore, where even the dead can't rest in peace; a publicity-conscious businessman turned feng shui expert; a professional feng shui man who became the most financially successful geomancer in Hong Kong.

Feng shui men today don't exactly fit the image of Mandarin sage—no long silk robes, no white wispy beards. When crew-cut Chen To-sang checks out a client's ancestor's grave, he dons bright yellow running shoes. Choi Pak-lai prefers well-cut three-piece suits. Although he occasionally sports a cotton mandarin jacket, Lin Yun generally garbs his portly shape in Hawaiian print shirts, black slacks, and slightly elevated shoes.

Black Hat Feng Shui

Tibetan Tantric Black Hat feng shui is practiced by only a handful of experts, among them Lin Yun. Black Hat feng shui is a hybrid of many customs, thoughts, and practices. It arose from the long journey of Buddhism from India through Tibet and finally to China. Along the way, it incorporated religious and philosophical theories, rites, and disciplines from the countries it passed through. From India it carried the word of compassion, the concept of *karma,** the practice of yoga, and the structure of an organized church, replete with proselytizing monks and religious ritual. In Tibet, it picked up magical and mystical knowledge and ritual such as chants and charms. After arriving in China, it was influenced by indigenous culture—yin-yang theory and Taoism, ancestor worship and animism, divination and feng shui, and even folk cures for every imaginable problem ranging from stomachaches to malign spirits, scholarly aspirations to childbearing, from attaining wealth and power to manipulating the destruction of one's enemies.

One outcome—Black Hat feng shui—is a practical eclectic version of feng shui, mostly based on intuition and mystical knowledge. Its feng shui cures are both logical—*ru-shr,* translated as "within our experience or knowledge"—and illogical—*chu-shr,* translated as "outside our experience."

---

*Karma: briefly, that one's destiny is determined by one's own good and bad deeds performed in this and past lives.

DIVINATION

One of the origins of feng shui was Chinese divination. The early Chinese used omens to decide on cures for sickness, sacrifices, and the advisability of war; to check out the hunting, farming, and fishing prospects; and to determine the auspiciousness of time and space.

One form of divination that influenced feng shui was astrology, a celestial model of cosmic order on earth. The emperor's palace in Ch'ang-an, the first capital of Imperial China, built in the third century B.C., was constructed, some say, in the shape of and along the astrological path of the Big Dipper—a particularly lucky constellation revolving around and pointing to the ever-stable North Star. Thus the emperor sat at the center of earthly power.

Divination and rituals are not new to the West. Before building any city, Greeks and Romans determined a site's suitability by inspecting the livers of animals grazing there to see if they were healthy. They also employed astrologers to ensure that the city was oriented in line with the cosmos. And like most Chinese towns, Western counterparts generally were laid out along a north-south axis.

But, more than astrology, feng shui was influenced by the pre-Taoist text the *I Ching or Book of Changes*. Growing out of a divining process using "oracle bones"—tortoise shells and ox shoulder bones that, when placed over a fire, cracked in several "yes" or "no" directions—the *I Ching* is the mother of Chinese thought and practices. It stresses the connection between man's destiny and nature.

By tossing coins, wooden blocks, or yarrow stalks, the Chinese interpreted omens, instruction, and wisdom from the resulting trigrams. These trigrams symbolize nature: ☰ heaven, ☷ earth, ☳ thunder, ☶ mountain, ☲ fire, ☴ wind, ☱ lake, ☵ water. They became symbols of other concepts such as family relations (☷ mother, and ☰ father), cardinal directions, time, and, finally, various stages of change.

The *I Ching* stresses a fundamental Chinese approach: constant cyclical change. Philosophically, it provides an overview of the universe as an entity and all things in it in constant flux. In fortune-telling, the outlook is never static: If circumstances are good, danger lurks around the corner; if luck is bad, things will look up—eternal regenerative change. Man floats with the ebb and flow of nature's tides.

I Ching symbols conjure up cosmic power and energy and are used as good luck charms and hexes. Printed on a cosmic compass, its trigrams provide feng shui men with eight bearings to properly align desks, doors, and buildings, setting man along a correct course in life.

TAOISM

Out of observation, identification, and dependency on nature came *Taoism* (pronounced ''dowism''), a philosophy based on the patterns of nature. Influenced by the *I Ching,* it defined man's relationship to the universe. The Taoists believed man was influenced by the cosmos, its topographical permutations, and its passages of time. By studying nature, the Taoists made contributions in scientific fields: astronomy, mathematics, geology, cartography, mineralogy, and chemistry.

The Taoists glorified nature. Love of nature permeated their view of life. Things would not be correct until man could mirror within the harmony of nature without. They exalted it in their poetry. Taoism ''seemed to answer the yearnings of men of feeling and imagination for a vision of the eternal in which they could forget the chaos of the present.''*

*Michael Sullivan, *The Arts of China,* rev. ed. (Berkeley, Los Angeles, and London: University of California Press, 1979), p. 96.

High rises the Eastern Peak
Soaring up to the blue sky.
Among the rocks—an empty hollow,
Uncarved, and unhewn,
Screened by nature with a roof of clouds.
Bringing up my life ceaseless change?
I will lodge forever in this hollow
Where Springs and Autumns unheeded pass.*

—*Tao-yun,* A.D. 400

Man's place in nature's enormous expanse and eternal change seems insignificant, "a drop of water in a flowing stream." Yet, he is also an integral part of the universe, swept along and controlled by its flow. This was expressed in the traditional landscape paintings of monolithic mountains looming over streams crossed by tiny human figures. It was at once a transcendental solace and a humbling thought to know you were part of a huge eternal structure.

Taoists perceive man and his surroundings as microcosms of the universe, *Tao.* Ideally, man should reflect the balance of nature. A third-century sage, Liu Ling, underlined this identification with the cosmos. Prone to lounging naked in his room, even when receiving visitors, he remarked to shocked guests, "I take the whole universe as my house and my own room as my clothing, why then, do you enter here into my trousers?"† Some T'ang dynasty poets would drink themselves into dreamlike stupors to unite and commune with nature. One eighth-century poet is said to have drowned when he reached out for the moon in drunken ecstasy.

Although remaining a philosophy, Taoism also became a popular religion. Prompted by the influx of Buddhism to China,

*Arthur Waley, *Translations from the Chinese* (New York: Alfred A. Knopf, 1941), p. 79.

†Feng Yu-lan, *A Short History of Chinese Philosophy* (New York and London: The Macmillan Company, 1948), p. 235.

Taoism adopted the trappings of an organized church: priests, rituals, and temples. To popularize Taoism and to compete with the growing appeal of Buddhism, Taoist priests also integrated native Chinese customs and wisdom: folklore, filial piety, sacrifices, astrology, herbal medicines, and feng shui. Hence, popular forms of Taoism and Buddhism became interchangeable. Even Confucian elements crept into Taoism, as many devotees prayed for scholarly advancement, offspring, and blessings from ancestors.

Unlike Taoist philosophy, the religion is worldly, more pragmatic than the Taoist philosophy. It deals with daily dilemmas rather than esoteric thought. Taoist priests use rituals to help believers achieve earthly comforts—social position, money, good marriage—preoccupations Taoist thinkers sought to transcend.

Along with its large repertoire of folk cures, religious Taoism adopted *I Ching* and Tao symbols to work as sacred charms. These potent religious symbols, while infused with Taoism's original message of an ever-changing universe, functioned as a precaution against earthly ills. Circling a mirror or a Tao symbol, *I Ching* trigrams create an amulet with mystical powers purportedly strong enough to ward off demons, disease, and other destructive forces from homes, shops, and temples. These charms operate in a manner similar to a Christian cross against vampires and devils or a dashboard Jesus against car crashes.

Though the seeds of feng shui were sown thousands of years ago, feng shui, as practiced today, grew out of both esoteric and popular forms of Taoism. Man's place in nature was to be in harmony. The Chinese used feng shui as a way of linking man's destiny with that of nature by placing graves, buildings, and people in what they divined to be a cosmologically auspicious environment.

Tao, of Taoism, literally means way, principle, process, or road. Tao is the eternal rhythm of the universe and how the universe works. It is also the way of man: Both the universe and man obey the same natural law. From early times the Chinese saw the cosmos as a way, a moving pattern. And that way was Tao.

Tao's roots spring from the Chinese people's witnessing the cyclical seasonal changes from summer to winter to summer again and the daily replacement of the sun and the moon—opposites continually spawning each other, constantly changing yet eternally recurring. Opposites seem to flow from one another rather than to conflict. Tao unites everything, exemplifying the need of nature and man to bring all opposing forces into a fluctuating harmony.

Tao connotes both a doctrine and a process. In the sixth century B.C., Confucius used Tao to preach the moral way or social order, emphasizing political and bureaucratic responsibilities. At roughly the same time, Taoist philosophers, such as Lao-tse, reacting to Confucius, used Tao to express the way of nature, urging people to return to the simple life and thus to return to the original harmony with nature.

Taoism offers a philosophical genesis. Lao-tse said, if opposites do indeed spawn each other, if summer gives way to winter, then reality must have sprung from nonreality: Before there was an *is*, there was an *is not*: a big void, a unity in nothingness, or a cup—maybe it is empty, maybe it is full, but it is undifferentiated. As Lao-tse wrote, "It was from the Nameless that Heaven and Earth sprang; the named is but the mother that rears the 10,000 creatures...."*

To balance the environment, feng shui men must determine the patterns of Tao. Two Taoist concepts—*yin-yang* and *ch'i*—guide the Chinese in establishing cosmic harmony on earth.

Yin and Yang

Yin and yang, the two primordial forces that govern the universe, symbolize harmony. They are opposites. Yin is dark, yang is light, yin is passive, yang is active. Yin is female, yang is

---

*Arthur Waley, *The Way and Its Power* (New York: The Macmillan Company, 1958), p. 141.

Yin-yang symbol.

male. In the *I Ching,* yin is —— , yang is —— . But, unlike Western ideas of conflicting extremes, yin and yang are complementary. They depend on each other. Without dark, there is no light. Without hot, there is no cold. Without life, there is no death. Like a magnet's positive and negative poles, yin and yang unite.

All things contain varying degress of yin and yang. Yin and yang continually interact, creating cyclical change. Some describe this ceaseless change as the swing of a pendulum: Winter gives way to spring, only to return in a matter of months; heat replaces cold, which gives way to heat; night follows day, which reemerges after some hours of darkness. There is a sense of wholeness in the movement of yin and yang. And the natural process that unites the two is Tao.

Lin Yun explains Tao's process:

> Yin and yang merge together into one—naturally and constantly creating Tao, the universal situation. The moon

(yin) comes out and as it recedes, the sun (yang) rises, then sets equaling one day, and this moon-sun interplay goes on naturally, creating the Tao of heaven and earth. The Tao of couples is when a woman and a man get married and become a family, giving and receiving with each day. Or luck can be rotten and then improve, becoming man's fate and fortune which is never constant, but fluctuates, sometimes good, sometimes bad. This is the Tao of man.

In Chinese traditional medicine, the body needs to maintain harmony. The Chinese say the inside is yin and the exterior is yang. When something goes wrong, the Chinese doctors say they can trace it to an imbalance of one of the principles. If you have an upset stomach (yin) and you feel nausea, your mouth will open (yang) and you will vomit—then you will feel better. This applies also to the emotions. If your heart or mind is upset or uneasy, you might cry; or if you are angry, you might yell. People's personalities must also have a complementary amount of yin and yang to get along harmoniously in marriage and in work.

In feng shui, the yin and yang of a house or a gravesite must be balanced, bringing residents into harmony with their environments.

Ch'i

Ch'i is the most important component of feng shui. One feng shui expert wrote: "If a geomancer can recognize ch'i, that is all there is to feng shui." Ch'i is the vital force that breathes life into animals and vegetation, inflates the earth to form mountains, and carries water through the earth's ducts. Ch'i is a life essence, a motivating force. It animates all things. Ch'i determines the height of mountains, the quality of blooms, the extent of potential fulfillment. Without ch'i, trees will not blossom, rivers will not flow, man will not be. And while all things—hills, streams, trees, humans, stones—inhale ch'i, they also exhale it, thus affecting each other.

The character ch'i.

Ch'i is a pervasive concept in Chinese traditional arts ranging from acupuncture and medicine to feng shui and gung fu (commonly known as "kung fu"). It can include such diverse phenomena as the energy that moves waves; the source of fertile earth; what martial artists channel when striking powerful blows; what acupuncturists seek to activate with their needles; and even man's aura. For thousands of years, the Chinese have hired feng shui experts to divine, like architectural dowsers, where the best ch'i flows in the landscape.

Mentioned as early as the *I Ching,* ch'i later blossomed as a neo-Confucian concept in the twelfth-century work of Chu Hsi. To the Chinese, ch'i links spirit and substance. Light ch'i floats as air; heavy ch'i sinks to form matter. "Ch'i is extensive and vague. Yet it ascends and descends, and moves in all ways without ever ceasing. That which floats upward is the yang that is clear, while that which sinks to the bottom is yin that is turbid."*

Ch'i follows the patterns of Tao, changing, condensing, and expanding, inhaling and exhaling. At times it is mass; at other times vapor.

In Chinese, the character *ch'i* has two meanings: one cosmic, one human. Heaven's ch'i encompasses air, steam, gas, weather, and force. Man's ch'i includes breath, aura, manner, and energy. The two types of ch'i are far from separate. Man's ch'i is strongly influenced by the ch'i of both heaven and earth.

The land most influenced by ch'i, the Chinese claim, is the most habitable: Flowers, trees, and grass grow fastest, animals are the fattest and most useful, and people are the happiest, most comfortable, and prosperous.

As Lin Yun describes it, ch'i spirals around and around in the earth, ever-changing; sometimes "exhaling" toward the crust, sometimes "inhaling" toward its depths, always pulsating and

---

*Wm. Theodore De Bary, ed., *Sources of Chinese Tradition* (New York and London: Columbia University Press, 1970), vol. 1, p. 468.

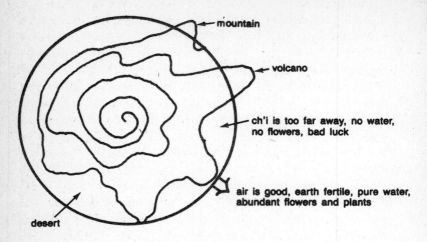

Ch'i and the world.

manifesting itself in different ways: a high mountain, a deep ravine, a flat desert. In the course of its turning, ch'i may rise near the earth's surface, creating mountains. It may expand so strongly as finally to escape, erupting into a volcano. And if ch'i recedes too far from the earth's crust, the land will be dry, desertlike, and flat. The best situation occurs when ch'i nearly brushes the earth's surface, causing mountains to form, trees to grow tall, grass to be green, air to be fresh, water to be clear, clean, and accessible, flowers to bloom, and man to live comfortably and contentedly. When ch'i is too far away, no water flows, pollution and sickness thrive, and there will be bad luck.

Atmospheric ch'i molds human ch'i. Ch'i must flow smoothly and near a person to improve his ch'i. It must be balanced. If the current is too strong or too weak, it can have negative effects.

From the fetal stage, human life is said to be closely linked to cosmic ch'i. This ch'i, in a sense, is a person's destiny. At conception *ling* (tiny airborne particles of ch'i), having entered a woman's womb, gives the fetus a spark of life. This is the embryonic form of the baby's ch'i. Ch'i pervades the whole body, determining a child's physical characteristics, movements, and mental state.

As with mountains and streams, the Chinese say, the human body is carried by ch'i, a central energy. Ch'i moves us, it causes contractions in muscles and tendons. The ch'i flowing out to the arms allows us, for instance, to bend our elbows, grasp and carry a cup, and sense hot and cold, thus warning of scalding things that might burn us.

Ch'i must flow smoothly and steadily through the body. If ch'i is too weak, we can't move. If it can't flow through an arm, that arm will be paralyzed. If ch'i doesn't circulate through the legs, they won't be able to walk, and if it doesn't reach the heart, then, without a beat, death will follow.

Human ch'i unites mind and matter. Ch'i is not just a signal telling us to move—*ch'i actually moves us*. Chinese painters stress the importance of the ch'i, or, roughly, the strength of the brush stroke. This creative ch'i flows through the body, the arm, along the brush, and then onto the paper or silk, linking artist with creation.

Ch'i, this breath of life, is man's aura, man's real self, his energy and soul. It can be seen by some. It propels us through life and affects our interaction with others. Because all people possess ch'i, every human movement influences both the self and other people. We have been said to give and receive all sorts of "vibes" and "chemical reactions." We are drawn together and repelled as magnets attract and repel. Whatever it is, we are sensitive to others' movements and manners, picking up intuitive information without words. In feng shui, people are also sensitive to the ch'i of their environment. Atmospheric ch'i shapes human ch'i, casting man's destiny. Feng shui practitioners try to direct a smooth, good current of ch'i to a person and divert or convert harmful ch'i.

aura

Buddha

shy,
reserved

after embarking on any
plan, he/she fails

suicidal,
self-defeating

jittery,
unchanneled ch'i

daydreaming

oblique personality, that is,
a flirtatious or shifty person

Human ch'i variations.

People possess different types of ch'i, producing various character traits, problems, and reactions. The most desirable is an even distribution of ch'i throughout the body and channeled through the head, creating a halo similar to the Buddha's topknot or Christ's aureole. Another ch'i might be less developed, hiding timidly in the body. Some people have slanted ch'i rising out of their shoulders—the ch'i of an extrovert, or someone continually distracted by his surroundings and opportunities.

A very pretty woman who walks into a crowded room but is not noticed has muted ch'i or presence, while a not-so-pretty woman with slanted ch'i in the same room would create a stir wherever she turned, striking other people's awareness (ch'i) with her ch'i and sending out strong vibrations.

Ch'i, although rooted in a person's body, may at times be directed toward a different time or place. The Chinese call that state, "The body is present, but the mind is not." We'd call it daydreaming. Those whose ch'i rises up to the throat, but no farther, can neither speak up, overcome trials, nor endure hardship. One whose ch'i comes out of the mouth before getting to the brain may talk too much without thinking about what he is saying. Another person's ch'i may be unchanneled, coming out from every which way, indicating a jittery, nervous disposition—a person who is frenetic about what he does without having any real impact or direction. Others may have good intentions, but when they enter society and the world, they fail—their ch'i rises toward the heart and falls limply out of the side of the body. Those with a downward moving ch'i will be self-defeating and suicidal.

Lin Yun begins to analyze people's ch'i by telling them to "look left, then right." Some people move just their eyes, others their heads, others their whole body. Some move smoothly but slowly, others in jerking motions, while others look left, then stop for a second, then look right. After diagnosing their ch'i, Lin Yun tries to help them "untangle" the knots inhibiting their happiness and effectiveness.

The Chinese admit feng shui has its limitations. Lin Yun says he can manipulate a person's destiny, but he can't change its general course. He says:

> Everyone has a potential and a fate. People are born being basically lucky, unlucky and medium lucky. That is fate. Sometimes you can't do anything to help a person—they may be slated to die. But usually, you can improve your lot to a point through initiative, discipline and feng shui to actualize your potential. So that a medium-luck businessman with drive and an auspicious office lay-out and building can financially surpass a good-luck businessman whose work space has less beneficial surroundings.

According to feng shui masters, buildings, trees, and sun all affect the quality and flowing of our ch'i, but do not increase or reduce the amount of ch'i in a person.

Feng shui's goal is to tap the earth's ch'i, just as the goal of acupuncture is to tap a person's ch'i. The feng shui adept must find a place where the ch'i flows smoothly and the principles of yin and yang are balanced. If this isn't possible, feng shui offers methods of bringing the environment into harmony. In divining the potential of a landscape, house, tomb, or room, feng shui experts discern if ch'i is expanding or receding and make suggestions accordingly.

The Chinese distinguish between yin and yang dwellings—the houses of the dead and the places of the living. Yin structures are morgues, mortuaries, and tombs. Yang builders include residences; offices; schools; shops; companies; public works, such as parks, airports, ferry piers, harbors, and train stations; urban planning features, such as bridges, roads, and buildings; and prospective projects with developmental possibilities, such as oil wells, factories, racetracks, and casinos.

Examining the feng shui of a building or grave generally requires a house call or visit to the tomb site. Like doctors, feng shui men will discern ch'i circulation and pulse. While some use cosmic compasses, others merely know where and how to look, sensing the luckiness of a site.

One seventeenth-century feng shui theorist wrote that recognizing an auspicious site requires special senses—a trained eye and a keen sensitivity.

> There is a touch of magic light... It can be understood intuitively, but not conveyed in words. The hills are fair, the waters fine, the sun handsome, the breeze mild; and the sky has a new light: another world. Amid confusion, peace; amid peace, a festive air. Upon coming into its presence, one's eyes are opened; if one sits or lies, one's heart is joyful. Here ch'i gathers, and the essence collects. Light shines in the middle, and magic goes out on all sides.*

*Andrew March, "The Winds, the Waters and the Living Qi," *Parabola Magazine* 3, no. 1 (1978), pp. 32–33.

Three

RURAL FENG SHUI

THE EARTH

To the Chinese, earth and cosmos comprise one "living, breathing
organism."[*] Feng shui men ascribe to nature not only cosmic
breath—ch'i—but also animal and human characteristics. A moun-

---

[*]Ernest Eitel, *Feng Shui: or the Rudiments of Natural Science in China* (Hong Kong,
1873), p. 20.

tain can be an awesome but benevolent dragon. An overhanging cliff might be a tiger's jaw. An hourglass-shaped rock might be an *amah* (nurse) or a maiden. Indeed, an entire branch of feng shui, the so-called school of forms, interprets the landscape by detecting shapes suggestive of animals or objects.

Feng shui is a language of symbols. And within feng shui vernacular, nature is a vast simile, an animal park with beasts wandering across it. The environment thus takes on a metaphorical quality: mountains can be watchdogs, tigers, or dragons; rivers can be dragons or serpents. But the metaphor continues, too, stressing the causal link between man and nature. Man is affected by these animallike earth masses, and these earth forms are endowed with the powers and attributes of the things they resemble. Nature imitates life: a dog mountain may guard, a tiger hill may threaten. Around one Hong Kong grave, a geomancer spotted elephant, snake, tiger, phoenix, and dragon mountains. The Chinese take this very seriously (we in the West also recognize mountains as representative of other objects: Camelback, Scarface, and even Nippletop).

The mere shape of a nearby mountain can cast an imprint on a person's life. In feng shui, like often produces like, and life can imitate nature. A mountain shaped like a calligraphy brush rest might spur scholarly success. A cliff on Lan Tao, an island off Hong Kong, resembles a naked man with an erection and is said to prompt exceptional flirtatiousness in the girls of a nearby village.

Shapes not only affect a person's character but can also threaten an area's prosperity. In the nineteenth century, crops repeatedly failed for several years in an area of China's Kwangtung province. Geomancers traced the source to some nearby hills resembling a rat, which they said was devouring the crops. Construction of a huge rattrap gateway was advised—and no sooner built than the crop yielded grain in abundance.*

*Maurice Freedman, "Geomancy," Presidential Address, London School of Economics and Political Science, 1968.

Mountain dragon.

Dragons, the most frequent mountain symbol, protect many Chinese villages. Different parts of the mountain mass embody aspects of a dragon. A line of ridges leading to the summit link the vertebrae. Ridges running to either side spread into arms and legs. Mountain streams and underground springs are veins and arteries pumping the earth's ch'i, the "dragon breath" or "dragon vapor." And to find ch'i one merely has to trace ridges of green foliage.

One Chinese commentator noted:

The magic dragon writhes and changes . . . and the mountain ridges that have life breath will start to run east then suddenly turn west, or begin to run south then suddenly head north. . . . Off they go in all directions. . . . It is said, if it [the landscape] has permutations, call it dragon: if it has none, call it barren mountain.*

It is no accident, then, that dragons figure largely in Chinese legend, art, and symbol. During the Ch'in dynasty, they became official imperial emblems, carved into thrones and embroidered on silk robes. The emperor, semidivine himself, was always termed a dragon: Many legendary emperors purportedly descended from dragon fathers. And with similar powers, mountain and water dragons rule their domains, warding off sickness, famine, and ill luck, and serving as creators and destroyers.

Hong Kong locals trace the name *Kowloon*, "Nine Dragons," to the unwitting self-sacrifice of the last Sung dynasty emperor. Legend has it that when the Mongol hordes invaded China, a seer advised the emperor to search in the south for nine dragons and there rebuild his empire. Arriving at the appointed place, he counted only eight mountains. In despair, the imperial dragon threw himself into the sea—having failed to include himself in the count.

*Andrew March, "The Winds, the Waters and the Living Qi," *Parabola Magazine* 3, no. 1 (1978), p. 29.

Though descriptions differ, the Chinese dragon is an odd mixture of several animals. One ancient claimed it had "the head of a camel, the horns of a stag, the eyes of a demon, the ears of a cow, the neck of a snake, the belly of a carp, the claws of an eagle and the soles of a tiger."* It is a versatile creature that can grow miles in length or shrink to the size of a bookworm.

But metaphors are more than mere figures of speech. The dragon embodied in myth the awesome forces of the landscape, most typically mountains, water, and wind. Hatched from precious stones called dragon's eggs, they served as both preservers and destroyers. They are an early attempt to explain not only natural forms but also natural forces on which the Chinese depended for their livelihoood and life. A water dragon, for example, when controlled, was the source of fertile fields; when unchecked, the source of death and destruction. Water dragons had the power over weather, tides, and water levels. To bring on nourishing rain, they merely flew to the clouds. The Chinese credited them with natural phenomena and disasters: An eclipse was caused by a dragon eating the sun and the moon; a storm was a dragon battle; a drought, a sleeping dragon; a flood, a wrathful one. To keep dragons happy, solicit their support, and thus control nature, Chinese traditionally sacrificed to rivers. Until the Han dynasty, young girls were thrown annually to river dragons as brides. The dragon image was so vivid in the Chinese mind that one was sighted as late as the sixteenth century. During a disastrous flood, one reportedly entered a home in northeastern China and escaped by bursting through the house wall, leaving a devastating hailstorm in its wake. The extent of dragon veneration grew to wasteful and absurd extremes: Po Chu-yi, a T'ang dynasty poet of the ninth century, and a governor known for his water-control projects, spurned dragon worship

*Donald Mackenzie, *Myths of China and Japan* (London: Gresham Publishing, 1939).

enough to write a satirical poem, "The Dragon of the Black Pool."*

Mountains and water are eternal in the Chinese mind. As landscape features of extreme beauty, they were havens transcending a fickle political world. Poets, painters, and scholars retreated to mountains and rivers. Turning away from upheaval and court intrigues, they looked to the landscape—translated as "mountain-water"—to find solace in Tao and contentment in nature's beauty. In city gardens, they withdrew from the outside world to the quietude of a miniature man-made landscape: Pools were lakes and rocks were hills, condensed forms of powerful mountains. As Tu Fu, an eighth-century poet, wrote, "The state may fall, but hills and streams remain."†

A country's feng shui depends on mountains and rivers. Lin Yun divides the earth into plains and hills and rivers and lakes: "By studying these resources, we can understand a nation's destiny," translated as "mountain-river."

Feng shui experts see mountains and water as interdependent: the keys to a Tao-like harmony within the earth, creating perfect vehicles to pump beneficial ch'i through the earth's veins. Mountains (yin or passive) are balanced by water (yang or active). Earth needs water to nourish crops; rivers need hills to avoid floods.

Mountains and water are thus two crucial features in feng shui. And the earth, of course, presents feng shui men with an endlessly varied terrain. In siting anything—a house, a village, a grave—they survey the shapes of the surrounding landscape. They examine the contours of mountains and the courses of streams. They look for specific good features such as orientation, trees, and rocks. They follow certain very basic rules and several classically auspicious settings.

---

*For the text of the poem, see Arthur Waley, *Translations from the Chinese* (New York: Alfred A. Knopf, 1941), pp. 166–167.

†David Hawkes, *A Little Primer of Tu Fu* (New York: Oxford University Press, 1967), p. 48.

Mountain peaks are the points where earth and heaven meet and from which all directions emanate. Temples and shrines dot Chinese mountains like telegraph stations to the gods. From the beginning of the Chinese empire, rulers made dynastic sacrifices on Mount Tai, the largest mountain east of Sian. They thus took possession symbolically of all quarters of the realm. A Han dynasty history, typically anxious to establish the Hans' right to rule, chronicles Ch'in Shih Huang Ti's failed attempts to ascend Mount Tai. It notes that because storms drove him from the peak, Emperor Ch'in was thus proven unworthy to rule. In contrast, the Han emperor Wu made several successful ascents.

Mountains served as axes in orienting houses and graves. This had its practical side. The north of a mountain is windy and shady; the south, calm and sunny; the east brings early morning sun; and the west faces the glare of dusk.

Hills have figured prominently everywhere in the world. The Chinese say that a house on the south or east side of a mountain is best; both house and vegetation will prosper under the sun's warm rays.

Auspicious spots also tend to lie close to the veins of subterranean ch'i, delineated by points—dragon pores—of rich green foliage and vegetation. These dragon veins usually run down the ridges and backs of mountains following the nerve network.

Certain topographic features make for bad feng shui. A flat riverless plain is devoid of ch'i. The Chinese warn against building a house on the tail of a dragon, because the dragon is in the habit of moving it, creating an unsettling situation. A house on the dragon's head can be risky: living on its brain is good, but a slight miscalculation could put the residents dangerously close to the beast's mouth, the source of strong ch'i and a huge appetite. Dwellers of a house sited under an overhang, or tiger's mouth, will always live in fear of being gobbled up, disappearing when his upper jaw drops.

A hill resembling a wide couch will bring early violent deaths to male offspring. A mountain shaped like an upside-down boat will bring illness to daughters and jail sentences to sons. The worst mountain forms range from turtles to baskets, from "eye of a horse" to ploughshare.

When natural contours are lacking, thoughtful altering of the earth is encouraged. Straight rivers, threatening life, money, and prosperity, can be turned to a more advantageous direction.

A protective mountain dragon, of course, needs plenty of clear water to drink. Lao-tse wrote, "The highest good is like that of water. The goodness of water is that it benefits its 10,000 creatures."* Such advice encouraged people to imitate the clear, pure properties of water. A large stream or river meandering along the earth's contours is integral and desirable to the feng shui landscape, dispersing smooth, advantageous ch'i. Water, often synonymous with money, is the life source not only of dragons but also of tigers, phoenixes, and tortoise mountains. The yang element in a landscape, water, according to Lin Yun, is moved by ch'i.† Ch'i rolls a river's waves, determines its course and currents, and defines its clarity and depth.

By merely looking at the flow of water, feng shui experts like Lin Yun can discern the nature and strength of ch'i. The shape of a lake, the twists and loops of a watercourse, and the speed of its current are all vital signs in discovering aspects of ch'i.

The Chinese have countless rules about the shapes and orientation of waterways. For example, a house built near the confluence of streams will prosper. Water should be balanced, not flowing too swiftly or too slowly.

But lifegiving water can also be destructive to feng shui. According to the ancient *Water Dragon Classic*, "Water must not be fast or straight. . . . If water pours out [of the site] it drains off, it is hur-

---

*Traditional Chinese feng shui books say, "Wind disburses ch'i, water retains it."

†Arthur Waley, *The Way and It's Power* (New York: The Macmillan Company, 1958), p. 151.

ried. How can it be abundant and wealth accumulate? If it comes in straight and goes out straight it injures men.'' If water runs fast and straight, not only will the area fall victim to arrowlike ch'i or ''killing ch'i'' but also the land unscathed by the river's ch'i will not enjoy much ch'i because it whizzes by so fast. Ch'i influence, in that case, is confined and directed to the current's line of fire. Sharp bends also project arrowlike ch'i.

Trees further improve a feng shui landscape, protecting against malign winds (or killing ch'i) and fostering good growing ch'i. Feng shui trees, specially planted, tend to be large and old. In Chinese poetry, the evergreen symbolizes longevity. Lin Yun says the greener the tree, the stronger the ch'i of the area. In rural quarters, abundant foliage signifies prosperity and is a sign to farmers of fertile soil. Stones, too, can be important. The Chinese sometimes feel the destinies of certain individuals are wrapped up in particular stones. These stones are large and oddly shaped and are often adorned with petitions to the gods.

What, then, makes the classic feng shui site? Most experts agree that the protective ''armchair'' hill formation, also known as

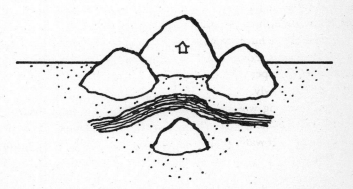

Classic mountain formation.

"dragon-protecting pearl" or "mother-embracing-child," is ideal. The armchair might be composed of a pack of powerful earthly beasts: the green dragon, the white tiger, the black tortoise, and the vermilion phoenix. The best site is backed by a high black tortoise mountain, flanked to the right by the fierce white tiger and to the left by a slightly higher green dragon—to keep the tiger's appetite away from the site—and, facing the lower vermilion bird, a sort of footstool to the armchair formation. The tortoise, tiger, dragon, and phoenix, in addition to retaining and emitting their own ch'i, snare the good ch'i flowing over the phoenix. Ideally a house would be built halfway up the black tortoise mountain, neither too high (yang) nor too low (yin), and looking over the phoenix with a commanding view.

Human needs and desires often conflict with ideals of natural harmony. Altering the land in any way—building a road, installing a well or swimming pool, constructing a house—can disrupt the currents of ch'i.

In premodern China, any changes to the land required feng shui men. Like doctors, they determined where an incision should be made and described what needed to be done to restore the balance of all earthly elements and yin and yang. The aim was always to bring earth and new constructions into harmony with the natural rhythms of the universe.

In a sense, then, the Chinese were early environmentalists; to violate the earth was heresy. They would avoid building a super-highway tunneling straight through the hills. Besides piercing the earth's flesh, straight roads conduct ch'i too quickly for anyone's good. Traditional Chinese roads thus wander slowly along the land's contours, avoiding any disturbance to nature's balance and tranquility.

One man's "balance," however, can easily be another's "blasphemy." Twisting and winding along every earthly deviation to avoid rupturing the earth, the Great Wall itself seems a classic of feng shui. Yet some saw the stone boundary, snaking 2,300 miles across China to the Himalayan foothills, as counter to feng shui's principles.

In the last days of the Ch'in dynasty (221–207 B.C.), when the emperor died and the succession came into question, the honorable General Mêng T'ien and the heir apparent were stationed out in the western reaches of the Great Wall, then only recently completed. Uninformed of the ruler's death, they received a forged letter, purportedly from the emperor. The letter, a product of the dead monarch's eunuch adviser, Chao Kao, who sought to establish his own puppet, accused Mêng T'ien and the heir of treason, and demanded their deaths. Imperial records tell of a parting soliloquy, in which Mêng T'ien bemoans the unjust accusations, then realizes he indeed had betrayed his country by overseeing the construction of the wall. In severing the veins of the earth, he put his country agriculturally and politically in jeopardy. Indeed, a few years later, the dynasty fell.

But if roads or construction work upset the balance of yin and yang, the flow of ch'i, and the currents of wind and water, feng shui can, for the most part, restore them.

The Chinese are fiercely protective of their surroundings, and this has often made problems for Western colonialists. Take the fate of poor Señor Amaral, a nineteenth-century governor of Macao, the Portuguese colony forty miles west of Hong Kong. Señor Amaral, it is said, combined a passion for road building with a contempt for Chinese superstitions and especially feng shui. He doubtless interfered with many Chinese tombs, but when he finally severed one too many dragon's feet, his own head was lopped off by an assassin. (The murder, the Chinese claimed, was the revenge of feng shui.)*

Feng shui, as it was practiced by Chinese peasants through the

*Eitel, *Feng Shui*, p. 2.

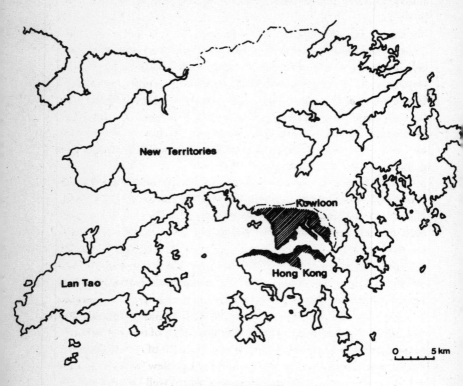

*Map of Hong Kong
and the New Territories.*

centuries, is still very much alive in Hong Kong's New Territories. Today, the Hong Kong government seems acutely aware of feng shui, especially in the rural areas. Before beginning housing projects, factories, and public works, or resiting villages or graves, district officers or corporate planners consult with village leaders. This derives primarily from the nature of Hong Kong's New Territories. Leased to the British in 1898 for ninety-nine years, the 400-square-mile area is probably the only large section of the China mainland openly to maintain a traditional rural Chinese way of life. Squeezed between ragingly capitalist Kowloon and the stridently communist People's Republic, the New Territories areas have somehow escaped both New China's four modernization programs and—for now—Western urbanization.

While Hong Kong and Kowloon—together one of the British Empire's last outposts—are technically as English as Kew Gardens, the New Territories has remained traditionally Chinese and essentially autonomous. For more than eighty years, the British have carefully maintained a "hands-off" policy. Officials defer to village elders, the clan heads who still make most major decisions. While the Red Guards were destroying Taoist and Buddhist temples just across the border, New Territories families such as the venerable T'angs, who trace their local roots to a Sung dynasty princess who fled there in the eleventh century, retained much of the architecture, customs, and beliefs of old rural China. (In light of recent Chinese-British talks about the Chinese reclaiming the New Territories after the lease runs out in 1998, rural feng shui might well become ancient history.)

The day-to-day problems in the New Territories are not unlike those of General Mêng T'ien, albeit on a slightly smaller scale. They range from altering the landscape for the worse to cutting off feng shui site lines to disturbing graves and their resident spirits.

Building roads is a particular problem. The government or developer can't blithely clear land and cover it with asphalt, because he just might cut a capillary of a dragonlike mountain.

In 1963, at Taipo's Plover Cove, where the British first raised the Union Jack over the New Territories in 1898, construction on a mountainside caused great complications. Digging into the earth revealed red soil, which to the villagers was the raw flesh of a wounded dragon. "When it rained," remembers John Warden, Secretary of the Home Office of the New Territories, "it was particularly unnerving to have blood-like mud gushing down from the hill-side wound." In similar cases, villagers had cut branches and brush to dress earthly wounds. This time, to calm the distraught villagers, a 100-by-200-foot fence was constructed, a bandage to spare them the gory sight. Sound odd? Well, maybe, but in the West, community groups band together to protect their environment. They raise a storm over development projects that might damage local trees and hill scarp. Instead of feng shui, it's often called "zoning."

Feng shui often seems logical to Hong Kong bureaucrats. Robert Upton, Assistant Regional Director of the New Territories, says: "From our point of view it also makes good sense to preserve park space as a wooded hill in the center of town. The villagers' insistence becomes our willing concurrence. What they're saying is sensible but it's a slightly different approach."

Sometimes even building techniques are altered to avoid feng shui conflicts. In one New Territories area, the builder used concrete blocks instead of driving stilettolike piles into the earth to construct a house.

The wonder is that anything gets accomplished. Most projects in the New Territories are preceded by an elaborate Tun Fu ceremony, an all-purpose ritual to placate any dragon or tutelary spirit in the area. Villagers say that without this something bad could happen.

In 1972, for example, because of a road the government proposed to build over their guardian mountain, villagers threatened to move from an area inhabited by their ancestors for ten generations. They explained: "If the dragon's neck of our feng shui is cut, our good fortune will vanish, then bad luck will come." More than forty-five years before, they noted, the people of Ting Kau village were all killed because the dragon air there was destroyed.

So every year the colonial government of Hong Kong doles out tens of thousands of dollars to appease not only local spirits but also villagers concerned over construction projects, swimming pools, roads, latrines, to mention a few. Most of the money goes into the Tun Fu ceremony. Taking a hard line, Mr. Upton says, "We give them a standard rate of about U.S. $1,500 and tell them to get a feng shui *lo* ["priest" in Cantonese] of your choice and say we'll be back next week with 'dozers." Often the government checks up on the town to see that their feng shui contribution is put to good use. A typical one was detailed by a Mr. Grout (see Appendix 1).

Sometimes, though, the Tun Fu isn't enough. After a winding path was terraced into a mountainside in Saikung Park, several local residents died. In a panic, the villagers called the Hong Kong government, complaining that the path had cut into a dragon. The government covered the path with turf, and all was well.

Cries of dragon molesting can sometimes be mere feng shui blackmail. Government officials say that the standard rate for Tun Fu ceremonies is sometimes an incentive to villagers to be feng shui hypochondriacs. Says Mr. Warden: "A large part of the Tun Fu money goes into the pockets of the village elders. Still some have objections of feng shui out of genuine fear. Yet feng shui is an indefinable thing people use as a ploy to squeeze the government out of money."

Eventually the government officers become pretty savvy about detecting such extortion. "You'll come across a villager who will say, 'Look, I don't want to hear about money, but my ancestor's grave is there and it's staying there.' That sort of thing," explains Mr. Upton. "On the other end of the scale, they'll say 'Can't be moved,' so you say, 'U.S. $1,200.' 'Can't be moved,' '$1,400.' 'Can't be moved,' '$1,600,' pause, '$1,700?' 'Done!'"

Mr. Upton says he and his colleagues caught on after a while to some basic feng shui rules. Analyzing natural forms, for instance, isn't difficult. With a slightly trained eye and an active imagination, the uninitiated Westerner can discern dragons from the landscape. In fact, many Chinese and British government officials in Hong Kong have become amateur feng shui los.

In 1977, when the government presented a New Territories village with a road proposal, the villagers balked. The road, they said, would chop their dragon's toes, making him uncomfortable, irritable, even vengeful. An official well versed in the subtleties of feng shui noted that if the villagers inspected the map closely, they'd see the road would not sever the dragon's toes, but merely clip its toenails, thus doing both the dragon and the locals a great service. The road, he said, would ultimately improve their feng shui.

As a compromise, the government agreed to build an altar on a hill overlooking both the village and the road. Such shrines generally enhance the feng shui, not only for their spirit-placating value but because their shapes harmonize with the landscape. Pagodas, indeed, are said to serve as lightning rods for cosmic ch'i.

One government architect is considered something of a feng shui wizard. In a park on Hong Kong Island, he designed an octagonal hilltop pagoda that, in addition to summoning the powers of the *I Ching*'s eight trigrams, is also said to disperse the exceptionally strong and harmful ch'i that blows from the north. His pagoda is credited with a business boom that occurred shortly after.

The Chinese see houses as important additions to the landscape. Pagodas of varying scales, replicas of a balanced universe, enhance their gardens. Landscape paintings generally depict a mountainside retreat—sometimes large temple complexes—lodged among mountains and waterfalls. Indeed, feng shui shared this tradition, as long as the dwelling not only fit into the environment but also enhanced the natural patterns.

Ironically, protective feng shui can also cause death and destruction. One feng shui stone sat in a river in China, wrecking countless boats every year. The locals wouldn't move it or diminish its size, fearing worse calamities might ensue.

Often feng shui stones get in the way of progress and enterprise. As George Stevenson, a Hong Kong solicitor, explains,

> In Saikung, New Territories, there was a rock on a village elder's land and someone tried to move it. Very soon afterwards, his eldest son drowned at sea. So it gathered an aura of bad joss. When we came along and tried to buy the land and offered to move the rock to another place—so we could build a multi-level carpark—he just wouldn't budge. He said if we moved it his next son would die, so we had to go around it.

Sometimes even houses can be less important than preserving feng shui. Problems arose when the New Territories administration wanted to widen a small road into two lanes. "But, there are lots of old buildings close to the road," says Mr. Upton.

> So at one stage we wanted to bring one lane down south, leaving part of the village in a loop, that way we didn't have to knock down any houses. A neat plan. But, woe and disaster, we found we were right in the middle of a feng shui area—a little wooded knoll, a stream, a little shrine and even a feng shui rock. The full gamut. We couldn't avoid it. So the road alignment reverted to the original proposal which meant knocking down people's houses. We've lost at least six months and several hundred thousand dollars [Hong Kong dollars], and if we have to move more than a few houses, it may be in the millions. Needless to say this wouldn't be the way it is done in England.

Siting is generally very important. Living in the wrong place may bring disaster. Back in the early part of this century, one entire village resited itself because no village male had ever attained the age of forty-five years and no chicken would live there; obviously, the feng shui was bad. Although the villagers were very poor, they expended a lot of money, time, and labor. Through their own effort, they moved from one side of a valley to the other side. After they moved, the men lived to ripe old ages and the chickens never strayed far from their coops.

Feng shui has its scientific basis. The value of watercourses dates to around 3500 B.C., when the Chinese became the world's first rice cultivators. To the rice farmer, a meandering river is a natural blessing, providing better irrigation and a more fertile soil silt than a straight rushing torrent. Such conditions produce larger, perhaps tastier, crops, allowing a family to be healthier and more prosperous—the origin of feng shui's link between water and money.

Using north-south orientation, the feng shui man takes advantage of solar power to heat homes. In China, entire Neolithic villages often faced south. The Chinese traditionally protected the houses against north winds by nestling them against the natural windscreen of a northern hill, or by building a wall with no northern gate. In Hong Kong's New Territories, villages today still generally follow these rules. The one modification is that most are not sited on mountains, but rest at the foot of the hills so workers can be closer to crops. In those cases, a band of special feng shui trees may separate the village from the hill.

Although an area may be totally deforested, often a grove of trees is left standing for feng shui reasons. The trees either serve as a wind barrier or assume potent mystic meaning. This tradition is so strong that even in the People's Republic, where officials say feng shui is ''backward'' or ''superstitious,'' such trees are an important fact of life and livelihood. Throughout the countryside of Guilin are barren hills stripped of trees by lumberers. Here and there, however, stand fully treed hillsides, always with a farm at their base. A Chinese guide pointed this out as evidence of feng shui, saying the farmers refused to let the government cut the trees. This practice is actually useful since it provides fine protection to the houses. It prevents soil erosion and dangerous mudslides from the hill, and acts as a windscreen to homes and crops. This same situation can be found in other more modern farming communes throughout China.

Practical value aside, though, feng shui trees are also guarded, often for centuries, to avoid the disasters that might follow any damage. So strong were such feelings that, in late nineteenth-century China, the high price of camphor wood used in shipbuilding was directly blamed on feng shui:

> The population from among whom the timber is procured is influenced to so great an extent by the feng-shui superstition that large offers are necessary to induce them to come forward with supplies. (*Peking Gazette,* January 1, 1877)*

Rural feng shui is riddled with superstition. Some trees and stones gather a mystique and are worshiped as wayside shrines. In Hong Kong, the branches of an old evergreen will often be festooned with petitions to the gods. Such trees are also found in Singapore, where massive urban-renewal programs often stop for nothing. In the middle of Singapore's old Chinatown stands an ancient gnarled tree. Although the area has been cleared for renewal, amid the rubble the tree remained, tended by an old man and covered with red paper and incense sticks. Says one Singapore resident, "There was a great hue and cry, so the bulldozers carefully circled the tree. They flattened everything for hundreds of yards around, but left it standing like an oasis in a desert. They're perfectly happy to knock down thousands of people's houses, but they wouldn't touch that tree."

In Hong Kong, sometimes feng shui trees aren't old, but are grown as protection against newly created malign spirits—tall buildings, smoke-belching factories, roads—or as a village boun-

---

*Stephan Feuchtwang, *An Anthropological Analysis of Chinese Geomancy* (Vientiane, Laos, 1974), p. 128.

dary and a hedge for privacy. Often when factories of new highrises are built near a farm or a town, the locals react by growing trees to block out the towering building's ill effects, or to neutralize pollution or bad ch'i.

(In some feng shui practices, however, trees and plants can be undesirable. They are seen as havens harboring malign spirits that are waiting to snare a person's health. On Cheung Chau, one of Hong Kong's outlying islands, a Western journalist returned to his newly rented cottage to find the surrounding trees and flowers chopped down, replaced by a layer of cement. His landlord, who lived upstairs, explained that the vegetation was a breeding ground for the evils that might befall his family.)

It is not unusual for a feng shui man to use rudimentary science to find a good site, then clothe his selection in mysticism. In siting a brick kiln, a feng shui man decked out in a saffron-colored robe set up a table with wine, burning incense, and religious paper. Despite the mystical trappings, the priest was actually divining the site not through communion with the gods, but by careful use of the scientific method. He discovered by watching incense smoke the general direction of the wind, then calculated the angle needed to blow it away from the village. By lighting religious money, he could estimate how high ashes flew and determine how high the stack should be.

Orientation eventually became more sophisticated and mystical. The world's first compass was invented in China not for navigation but for geomantic purposes. Some feng shui men today use an intricate version of this same compass, with all the elements of the Chinese universe charted in, sometimes as many as twenty-four concentric circles around a lodestone. The outcome, putting it simply, is the harmonizing of the perfection of the universe with the earth.

This way of siting can be very exacting. Take the Tin Hau Temple in the center of Tsuenwan village in the New Territories. The 200-year-old structure obstructed the Mass Transit Railway tracks. Villagers insisted the temple was Tsuenwan's good feng shui, and that because of it the town had developed quickly into a prosperous area. A compromise was struck: While the temple would be moved to let the railroad be built, it would later be reconstructed, brick by brick, in the same place, facing the same direction (west). The price: U.S. $400,000.

Although the compass is a traditional feng shui tool, today some geomancers find they can do without it. Says Lin Yun, "I have internalized the compass."

GRAVES

Hong Kong graves seem to sit on the best plots of land. Hundreds of graves populating Hong Kong's mountains enjoy views of lush greenery, the South China Sea, and islands that seem to rise abruptly out of the glimmering water like the backs of whales playing in the bay.

For thousands of years, the Chinese, from emperors to field laborers, have applied great thought and money to the selection of gravesites. They believed that unless the deceased were properly buried the descendants would suffer. The offspring of an ancestor with an exceptionally good grave, it is believed, will be rewarded with wealth, health, lots of sons, and perhaps even a high position.

Graves, insists Chen To-sang, a feng shui man in Hong Kong, are the most important feng shui considerations. He blames the deaths of John F. and Robert Kennedy, for instance, on "an ill-placed grave—definitely a grandfather's tomb has bad feng shui." Using the same line of reasoning in 1979, he predicted that Teddy Kennedy would never be elected president.

Gifted with hindsight, Lin Yun traces the United States' myriad problems to the relatively insignificant-looking grave of its founding father, George Washington. Besides being sited too low into the foot of a hill at Mount Vernon, the tomb's entrance is shaded by a large tree planted several feet in front; thus lack of sun and limited ch'i flow hinder the country's development.

The feng shui of graves is wrapped up with the age-old Chinese practice of ancestor worship. The rewards are the impetus to maintain the ancestor's grave. One nineteenth-century missionary denounced the practice as un-Confucian and selfish.

In siting a grave, feng shui men use many of the living siting methods. The area's outside influences must be surveyed: whether the grave is close enough to a body of water; whether the orientation is correct, with the green dragon to the left and the white tiger protecting the right flank, the black tortoise in the back, and the red phoenix in front. Burials have been delayed for months while the perfect site was sought.

One geomancer retraced Sun Yat-sen's rise to his mother's well-placed grave in Clearwater Bay, New Territories. The grave follows the classic feng shui strictures. It sits on the south side of a tortoise looking out on the blue water of the South China Sea. To its left is a mountain, the green dragon; to the right sits a lower hill, the white tiger. Besides the embracing hills, the view and the site of a water body, symbolizing money, are also important. Some people buy up land in front of their graves to ensure against buildings blocking off its access to wealth.

Mountain shapes can influence the deceased's descendants. A misshapen mountain can bring misfortune. One Chinese-born American links literal deformity to a cleft in a hill facing the ancestral gravesite. "Since we started burying there," she explains, "each generation gave birth to one child with a harelip."

Sometimes, in grave siting, a grain of science exists. The area north of Loyang has long been famous as a burial ground, principally because the low water table kept the corpses dry and prevented decomposition, thus, the descendants thought, preserving family fortune and wealth.

Stories and legends proliferate about the marvels and power of feng shui graves. Back in the Ming dynasty, they say, a man became emperor by hanging his father's coffin in a mountain cave—the mouth of the dragon—so the father literally became the dragon's tongue.

Besides its offspring, the fate of a nation depends, it is said, on the correct burial of the ruler. When ill befalls a country, the source may be not the economic or political policies but a wrong siting of a ruler's grave. Some Chinese say Taiwan's political problems, especially the United States' recognition of the People's Republic of China in 1978, are linked to the incorrect placement of the generalissimo's grave: on a living dragon instead of a dragon for the dead.

People are not beyond using the dead to hurt their enemies. About fifty years ago in Taiwan, people attributed the rise of a rich family to the good placement of the father's grave by an artful feng shui professor from China. The family prospered and had lots of sons, who in turn prospered until the feng shui man's son came to Taiwan and was ill-received by the family. To punish their ungratefulness, he bought the land in front of the grave and planted a semicircle of bamboo trees with a road joining the ends of the grove and another perpendicular road aimed toward the grave, like a bow and arrow. Strangely, the gravestone cracked in half. Within three years, the family went broke and many of them died. So they hired another feng shui man from China to see what had gone wrong. He discerned the problem, and set it right by replacing the headstone and placing two stone rabbits on either side of the grave with their hands out, ready to catch the arrow (rabbits are quick). In a year, all was well.

Graves are the oldest surviving example of feng shui in China. Like the Egyptians, when burying dead royalty the Chinese took great care to create an environment where the dead might rest forever as peacefully and comfortably as possible. The grave of Ch'in Shih Huang Ti, the first emperor of China, is a man-made mound of earth arranged along a north-south axis with a life-size army flanking the tumulus. In fact, a palacelike design was re-created in the vault. The product of 700,000 laborers, the tomb interior represented the harmony of the universe, with heavenly constellations painted on the ceiling and the earth's topography complete with mechanically run quicksilver rivers and oceans on the floor. (In earlier dynasties the safety and comfort of a dead ruler were ensured by burying human attendants, chariots, horses, and decapitated enemies.)

If the grave escaped looters, the inside would reveal favorite artifacts, frescoes of both courtly and religious processions, and coins, bronzes, and mirrors. Today, the Chinese carry on this earlier tradition of sending treasured objects to the spirit world by burning mansions, Lear jets, cars, servants, clothes, toilet articles, pots, pans, money, and sunglasses—all, of course made of bamboo sticks and paper. Other favorites of the deceased, such as cigarettes, are placed in the coffin.

A sort of immortality—a perennial pursuit of the ancient Chinese—was achieved in some imperial graves. In one Han dynasty princess' tomb, the geomancer must have found an adequately dry place to preserve for 2,000 years not only her body but the silk robe she wore on her funeral day.

One grave in the New Territories was so auspiciously placed that it remained intact for 300 years. Modern buildings have been constructed on lesser plots around it, and the horseshoe-shaped T'ang grave remains sitting on several acres of choice Tsuenwan real estate with a feng shui siteline to the sea. (The grave's shape itself is considered lucky, mimicking the mountain armchair formation.) The placement of graves in the New Territories has rewarded offspring financially. When government or private contractors want to construct a building or a road, they often have to pay high grave fees for exhumation and relocation, or sometimes they must even divert public projects.

Graves in the New Territories are like booby traps. Burial urns seem to mine the entire countryside. In Yuen Long, when the government wanted to surface a road "purely for the benefit of the villagers," they found a lot of burial urns containing dried and scoured bones. The descendants insisted that that road section not be disturbed, that it remain unpaved. Today the asphalt road has a rough ten-foot-long earth track.

Feng shui men grapple with siting graves even in Catholic and other Christian cemeteries. In all cases they must divine how best to use ch'i. The plot shape, according to Lin Yun, is important; it must attract and bring in ch'i. A square plot is best. It is also good to have a narrow inner part and a wide entrance.

A narrow entrance causes problems. "If the narrow section is at the entrance and the wide part at the back, this drastically influences the life, the career and financial opportunities of the sons and grandsons. Their road will become more and more narrow." The area must not have a closed, claustrophobic feeling.

As for the headstone, it must be placed like the grave's headboard. Maintenance, says Lin Yun, is important. Sometimes the gravestone can change color. If it blackens, catastrophe will befall the family. "If white comes out of the stone, the family within two or three years will have a white happening," claims Lin Yun. (White is the Chinese color of deepest mourning.) So, Lin Yun advises, you can either scrub the white or black off—a rational solution—or, even better, "use the *chu-shr*, transcendental way, and rub the white streak with either *jusha* [a red powdered medicine] or *jusha* wine."

A yin site should be drier than a yang site, so the body and coffin won't rot quickly. For this reason Lin Yun says a family should make sure the plot has good drainage to siphon off the rainwater and that the neighboring graves' drainage doesn't run into the plot.

Four

TOWNSCAPE FENG SHUI

The Valley Wind

Living in retirement beyond the World
Silently enjoying isolation,
I pull the rope of my door tighter
And stuff my windows with roots and ferns.
My spirit is tuned to the spring season:
At the fall of the year there is autumn in my heart
Thus imitating cosmic changes
My cottage becomes a Universe.*

*Lu Yün (262-303). Waley, *Translations from the Chinese*, p. 79.

Feng shui has its roots in the very beginnings of society. With plenty of sites to choose from, the first men to build houses naturally sought the easiest and most comfortable spots. Facing south, safely above floods, and sheltered from the north wind, man and his flocks thrived among warm sun, water, and abundant plants. Those with the best eye for such locations prospered.

In towns and suburbs, and even in the densest of cities, rural feng shui rules can—and do—work. The search for ch'i and the balancing of yin and yang are still the prime goals in the placement of houses. The Chinese in Hong Kong are quick to point out that previous colonial governments, knowingly or not, observed basic feng shui principles. Every feng shui man I consulted agrees that the governor's mansion, standing high above the heart of Hong Kong's financial district and Victoria Harbor, occupies one of the colony's most propitious spots. They say much of the colony's financial and political success can be traced to this seventy-year-old white building. Built when Hong Kong was no more than a small port town, the mansion's entrance faces not the harbor side, as one might expect, but the botanical gardens on the uphill side. This is said to help the governor make judicious and balanced policy. Says Chen To-sang:

> If he faced the water, it wouldn't be as good. You see, on the right side of the house is Victoria Peak—a dragon whose spine runs along through the garden to the entrance of the house. So the governor enjoys ch'i that practically goes to his doorstep. And as if this isn't good enough, another mountain arcs around so that, with the Peak, it protects the house, cradling it like the arms of an embracing mother.

With civilization encroaching on the landscape, inevitably some old beliefs must be discarded. The construction of roads, the disruption of graves or burial urns, or the moving of a certain stone—all crucial to village or farm life—become less important. The modern feng shui man faces a new environment. As more people move into an area, the number of choice spots inevitably declines: not every house can have a sea view, or be backed by a hill; defined plots and regular streets require new rules and variations on old ones. To all of this feng shui men have adapted. They must reconcile and exploit not just the traditional forces of mountains, trees, wind, and water but also the host of modern man-made forms: roads, sewers, plots and house shapes, neighboring houses, and even such esoterica as zoning.

As man's hand comes to dominate a landscape, architecture also plays an increasing role in the workings of feng shui. Despite all the talk of natural forms, traditional Chinese buildings did not, at least by Western standards, fit harmoniously into the landscape. In fact, from the second millennium B.C., Chinese homes, temples, palaces, and even whole cities followed formal geometric lines—a U-shape building complex squared off by a screen or surrounding walls. These rules were far from being arbitrary—they were symbolic and sacred. On one hand they might be seen as angular imitations of mountains, refined representations of the feng shui ideal generally set on a north-south axis. A good example is Erh Li-tou, a Shang dynasty (1766–1123 B.C.) palace in Henan province. The main building lies in the north part of the compound facing the entrance gate and therefore the sun. This layout might have been derived from the protective, archetypical formation of the mountain animals: red phoenix, black tortoise, green dragon, and white tiger. It sheltered residents from harsh northern winds.

Until recently throughout the empire, Chinese, be they prince or pauper, built houses along this same model with only slight deviations, using bricks of the same uniform measurements. If a family grew in size, they merely built on another square unit. Sometimes compounds encompassed half a dozen of these units.

Even contemporary, Western-trained Hong Kong architects admit to using basic feng shui concepts. Eric Cumine in designing the Hong Kong Country Club dealt not only with the property's man-made boundaries but also with its surrounding landscape, a mountain in back and the sea in front. "I tried to disguise the property lines and work with natural boundaries, balancing the area with bushes here and trees there." Thus, in relation to the plot, the clubhouse is askew, in line with only the natural elements. Says Mr. Cumine: "The best measured building drawings are unequal. Symmetry isn't necessary to have balance. Nature isn't symmetrical; our faces aren't symmetrical, our hearts aren't symmetrical."

HILLS

Hills have figured prominently in the development of towns everywhere in the world. While the West often used them to center towns and forts, for the Chinese they have traditionally been welcome barriers, defenses against Mongol barbarians and cold northern winds. Hills—or, in flat areas, mounds of dirt—were also believed to supply heat, making winter life more comfortable. As modern architects will confirm, they also retain coolness in summer.

The shape of a hill, which is a product of the powers of wind and water, is crucial in town feng shui. Seen as earthly outcroppings formed by good ch'i, hills present rich, useful imagery normally associated with rural areas: dragons, tigers, phoenixes, and the rest. (Unlike the countryside, though, Chinese towns and suburbs long ago surrendered to the man-made alterations in the landscape. Residents rarely erupt in protest or demand Tun Fu ceremonies at the first sight of a bulldozer.) The worst possible location for a building is featureless ground—a flat plain with no ch'i-formed undulations—probably because in ancient China such a house would be threatened by floods during spring thaws or heavy rains.

Looking at hills from the side, the Chinese see three basic shapes: round, square, or triangular. The gracefulness of a rounded hill and gentle valley is naturally the most preferable, offering a continuous rolling quality in its contours. Square buttes, with the house

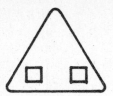

Triangular hill or plot:
Put house on the muscle of this
shell-like shape to hold in ch'i and money.

on top, will protect the house from floods, but expose it to cutting, harsh winds. Triangular land is inhabitable only if terraced, or if the house is sited at just the right place. If by chance a triangular hill resembles a mussel or clam shell, Lin Yun suggests building a house not on the hill's side, but in the place of the animal's tenacious muscle to hold in ch'i and money.

According to tradition, a Chinese house should be built in a commanding but well-sheltered place: midway up a hill facing south to the sea is the classic. In this case feng shui principles coincide with Western ideas of good location. "Some people who don't know about feng shui," comments Lin Yun, "still choose a good place to live." (Not surprisingly, these are often the rich, with beach houses facing the sea and backed by a mountain.) Best of all, though, is an armchair-shaped hill arrangement protecting the house on three sides—the so-called azure dragon, white tiger, black tortoise. A bad situation, on the other hand, might be under a bulge or an overhang—a "tiger's head" or "lion's head." It would be unwise to tempt such a beast by placing one's house under its mouth.

The preference for a protected site rather than an exposed hilltop has deep roots in the Chinese character. Unlike Westerners, who seem to try to dominate nature, feng shui followers seek to use it. Hong Kong Island with its thrusting mountains shows both sides of the dichotomy. To resident expatriates and some Westernized Chinese a symbolic hierarchy exists: The higher one lives, the better one's station, with the Peak itself the pinnacle of prestige. Many Chinese are amused at the wealthy corporate directors and diplomats residing in mansions, luxury highrises, and consulates on the Peak 1,500 feet up, usually shrouded in damp mist and buffeted by drafty wind, and a long trip from most offices and stores. Many wealthy Chinese prefer, instead, the comfort of mid-level flats, nestled against the mountain, often with better views, greater convenience, and protection from typhoons. (Lin Yun adds, though, that a house might be built on a hilltop, but only on a spot exceptionally well endowed with ch'i.)

In feng shui terms, of course, development often unbalances nature. Roads cut through mountain veins or high knifelike buildings plunge into the earth's flesh. In these cases, the keen eye of a feng shui expert has proved indispensable. Hong Kong architects, engineers, and contractors often seek their advice. Feng shui experts look beyond immediate landmarks for signs of danger or good luck. On Po Shan Road in Hong Kong, developers cut into the mountainside creating a flat terrace to build some luxury apartments. In 1975, a feng shui man perusing one of the flats warned its occupants they must move out right away: "There is a dangerous frog crouching on top of that slope," he said pointing to an overhang. "At any moment it might pounce." The family did indeed move, and a week later, after heavy typhoon rains, a "frog" of mud slid down the steep slope, burying their old building, and killing eighty neighbors.

Sometimes, though, the geomancer can improve the feng shui landscape. If a hill resembles a headless animal, a house built at the neck would place the residents in the position of thought and control. The house, by creating the head, not only completes a natural design, but also brings harmony to the landscape, enhancing its ch'i and the ch'i of the residents.

WATER

In town siting, as in rural feng shui, the topography of water, symbolizing money, is crucial. There can be too much or too little, and both are equally bad. A house at the head of a round bay is best because the water is round and money is balanced and flowing in; houses on the end of a point may have trouble, with nothing to hold the water/money in. Another good place for a house is above the confluence of streams. But a stream running through a yard, close to the house, emits bad ch'i and can carry away a family's fortune.

Ponds, lakes, or rivers in front of a house are generally good, bestowing ch'i on residents. But Lin Yun cautions that one must see if the waters are "alive"—clean and moving, activating pure and good ch'i—or "dead"—dirty and stagnant, damaging health, diminishing ch'i, and, incidentally, breeding mosquitoes. Dead water may also influence the way residents make financial ends meet by predisposing them to move toward tainted money. The Watergate complex, Lin Yun points out, is well placed in Washington, overlooking the Potomac River and its financially beneficial ch'i. Because the river water is polluted, though, the money could be sullied and various nefarious activities could occur.

As with all feng shui, a garden pond or pool must be balanced: It should be close enough for the house to benefit from the water's ch'i, but not so close as to be destructive or dangerous. Ch'i from the latter sort, says Lin Yun, will leap quickly from the water, hitting the house like a gun blast and causing "unfortunate occurrences." To lure in distant waters, Lin Yun prescribes hanging a mirror that acts as a magnet for ch'i. To modify the ch'i of a pond too close to the house, Lin Yun suggests lengthening the distance by laying a winding pathway from the pond to the house. This is similar to the meandering paths and archways and zigzag bridges in Chinese and Japanese gardens that prolong the spatial and temporal interval of getting from one point to another, artificially lengthening the land-

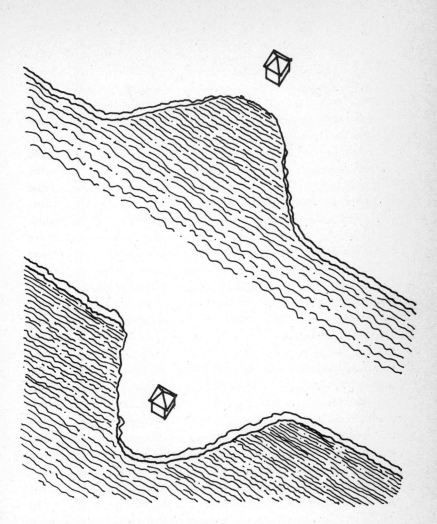

Water shapes: A house at the head of a bay is best, water and money flow in. A house on a point can be bad with nothing to hold money in.

scape vista and giving a small garden the appearance of being larger and symbolizing the universe in microcosm.

Size is also important, and should the pond be larger than the house, its ch'i may overwhelm the residents. Explains Lin Yun, "The most important aspect of the land should be the house where the people live, not the water. They are the hosts and the pond should be the guest. The guest shouldn't be larger than the host." To correct an awkward situation, Lin Yun will use a lamp, a rock garden, or a tree at the end of the yard opposite the pond. This, he says, balances the area, extending the domain of the house and disbursing the pond's excessive ch'i.

From ancient times, the Chinese stressed the water body's shape. The ideal was a quarter-moon-shaped pool circling away from the house. The feng shui of household wells is discerned through yin-yang analysis: well water (yang) ripples in the well (yin); people (yang) move through the house (yin). Therefore, in the digging of a well and filling it with water, yin is taken away and replaced with yang. In the house, the repercussion might be the illness or death of a person (yang) to balance the loss of yin outside. Lin Yun, in fact, says that the creation of a new well or window can bring sickness or death to a family. But he adds that, fortunately, old wells in existing houses are usually fine, provided the residents have not been having troubles.

A stagnant, poorly maintained well may become what Lin Yun terms "a reservoir of sorrow and bitterness." One cure is to place a plant on top to bring up bad ch'i and make it more positive. Sewers are also malevolent, but a cover near a house can be offset by placing a flowerpot filled with rice on the cover so the family will grow and eat well.

PLANTS AND TREES

Plants, as in rural areas, provide keys to the nature of an area's ch'i. Says Lin Yun: "Some have light shades, others are vibrant green, like newly sprouted grass. You can usually trace a line connecting all the bright green plants." Such lush stripes are often termed "dragon veins" or "green ribbons." Buildings sited at points along them enjoy first-rate earth ch'i, tapping the landscape's most positive energy. Similarly, an ivy-covered house almost always outshines one with only a scattering of foliage.

Trees can be both good and bad in town feng shui. For a house on the roadside, they hedge against pollution, noise, and bad ch'i from passing traffic. Especially when planted to the west, they will block the worst heat of the summer sun. But too close to an entranceway, trees can break up the flow of incoming ch'i and inhibit that of residents passing by.

Because of their tie-in to the flow of ch'i, trees are often viewed as omens. Indeed, some have traced Taiwan's ejection from the United Nations to the death of a huge oak, one of two that had guarded the front of its official residence (suitably named Twin Oaks). For more than a decade, the ambassador fretted, but took no action, as the tree slowly withered. Just when the tree finally had to be cut down, the embassy was asked to close in favor of the rival People's Republic. As Lin Yun comments: "If I had known of this then, I would have advised them to plant a larger, more expensive, and better oak in the dying tree's place."

ROADS AND STREETS

The feng shui access to a house should be cordial, not direct. The ideal is a pleasantly meandering approach, or at least a house off to the side of the road. By far the worst is the terminus of an arrow-straight dead end, the fast-flowing conduit of notorious "killing ch'i." Residents of houses skewered by straight-road ch'i may fall sudden victim to strange accidents and unexpected illness. Their friends will be untrustworthy and secretly critical, "stabbing" them in the back and "pointing" accusatory fingers. Such awful sites—and their cousins, the intersection of two perpendicular streets—suffer markedly in value in a Chinese town. In Singapore, for example, a house under the gun of a dead-straight street brought $50,000, $10,000 less than its virtually identical roadside neighbor. Ed Hung, managing editor of the *Hong Kong Star,* had a problem with a one-way road running down a hill straight at the entrance of his house. "The road was bad," he explains, "because headlights rushed at our gate like tigers stalking in the night." To defend themselves from the malign effects of the charging cars' killing ch'i, the family installed a fish pond in the small yard between the road and the house. Lin Yun adds that if a fountain or waterwheel were added, making the water ch'i rise, it would disburse even further the road's killing ch'i.

But a kind of opposite, draining effect can also damage a house's feng shui. Even a propitious house midway up a hill can have problems if its entrance drive leads straight down from the front door, allowing ch'i (and thus, money) to roll out. Another source of trouble is a too-narrow driveway, restricting the influx of ch'i. Far better is one that tapers toward the house, with the widest point where it hits the street to sweep in ch'i like a dustpan. John Chu, owner of a Hong Kong interior design store, is a connoisseur of street feng shui: "A fellow I knew lived at the top of a long hill, just the thing for money to flow out—and hardly the place for a bank manager. In the end, he was caught for embezzlement and killed himself jumping from the fourteenth story." Mr. Chu's own shop sits along a sloping road, but he sees no serious danger: "If you're in the middle, you can catch the money coming from stores farther up."

To lessen financial fallout from a hilltop home, Lin Yun suggests either moving the entrance to the side or installing a patio in front of the entrace. Even driveway shapes and directions are considered. One tapering Hong Kong driveway pointed straight toward its house like a dagger threatening its occupants. At the end of the driveway, they placed a white light to stabilize and equalize the ch'i flow. (The light, they confided, might steal their neighbor's ch'i so it would shine on them instead.)

NEIGHBORS

Nearby houses, like hills or bodies of water, can seriously affect feng shui. Happy neighbors, of course, are always a good sign, and even the best feng shui men will try to check them out. But as Lin Yun explains, crowded suburban neighborhoods can also bring problems:

> As other people discover the beneficial setting of a house with good feng shui, they too flock there, building their own homes. As more houses crop up, these buildings affect each other—one may be much higher or larger than another, another may obstruct the sunlight or view of its neighbor. As the surroundings of the original house change, the dwelling loses its peacefulness and security; it becomes unbalanced and the occupants may suffer.

The shapes of neighboring houses often present problems. A wealthy Chinese in Hong Kong—a self-made man with vast financial holdings, some in the United States—raised a hoopla over a local American family building a house right in front of his residence. Immediately cries of feng shui arose. Although the new house blocked part of his view of Hong Kong harbor and its money-giving power, the main offense was the new house's chimney. It was, he insisted, a nail being hammered into his coffin-shaped driveway, causing his financial downfall. Solutions were sought. He tried unsuccessfully to buy the house; the expatriate neighbors even consulted a feng shui man and offered to relocate the chimney, only to be turned down. "You would have thought he'd change his driveway shape," remarked the new neighbor. But, as they discovered, he was only looking for a scapegoat. "His son told us not to worry—that the old man had simply overextended himself financially and needed an excuse for his setback."

The neighbor problem cropped up for a Hong Kong jockey who couldn't win any races after moving to a new house. A horse owner's wife, very keen on feng shui, sent over her feng shui man. Just above the place, he noticed a very modern house, a white structure with brown glass around it. It resembled, he said, an open-mouthed frog—terribly bad luck. The feng shui man hung a mirror to reflect back the bad vibrations, and at the next races, the jockey managed two wins.

THE ALL-PURPOSE REMEDY

Mirrors are the aspirin of feng shui. Whether the problem is weak ch'i, or too much bad ch'i, nasty neighbors, a wrongly shaped room, a threatening highrise, menacing ghosts, or the infamous arrowlike road, the cure is often no more than the polished bottom of a wok or a bit of shining glass.

The mystic appeal of mirrors runs deep in Chinese history. Worn on the breast or shield of a feudal warrior, they were amulets to ward off enemies and demons. Hung inside and outside a house, they kept malign spirits at bay. Chinese archaeologists have found hundreds of mirrors buried in ancient imperial tombs. During the Chou dynasty (1122–256 B.C.), bronze mirrors were said to reveal not just faces or things, but much more: "The brilliance of the mirror represented the light of the sun and the moon combined: communicated the intention of the powers of earth beneath and the spirits in heaven above.''*

Mirrors today serve more prosaic uses. In Chinese communities throughout Asia and the world, they are the all-purpose solution to a vast range of feng shui ills. Most often, their use is defensive, an everyman's solution to easily visible threatening forces. In police stations, they are often hung to ward off corruption. For an expert, though, they can also be subtle, and Lin Yun places mirrors to balance poorly shaped rooms and even attract positive ch'i. Trial and error, though, is the way most people begin.

In a pinch, practically anything even halfway shiny will do. The ubiquitous *ba-gua*—a small, round mirror embedded in wood—comes plain (with I Ching trigrams only) or fancy (trigrams plus a menacing warrior god). Woks are a perennial favorite, apparently continuing to function even when covered with rust. Broken bits from an old medicine chest lack class, but will often get the job done.

Aware of reflective powers, people get very upset when evils are deliberately sent their way. Mirror wars are the result, and some have nearly ended up in court. One story starts with a Hong Kong family whose house had a feng shui deficiency. The solution was deemed to be a mirror with two menacing prongs sticking out. It was aimed, though, at a neighboring mansion, whose owners apparently had enough bad spirits already. They retaliated, installing a larger mirror with three prongs. For years the battle raged, each side putting up more and more mirrors. Finally the issue was decided by the police, who deemed the battlefield a hazard to nighttime motorists and ordered the armaments removed.

*Florence Ayscough, *A Chinese Mirror* (Boston: Houghton Mifflin, 1925), p. 9.

THE LAST RESORT

When absolutely nothing works—often because development has totally destroyed any chance of natural harmony—even the most imaginative feng shui man may give up and simply recommend getting out.

Lin Yun, though, is not traditional. His Black Hat mystical feng shui has evolved what he says are remedies for even the most hopeless cases. These "secret ritual practices" are mystical methods of manipulating and correcting feng shui. Unknown to traditional feng shui experts, these cures follow a transcendental, irrational, and subconscious healing process known as *chu-shr*, or that which is outside our realm of experience or knowledge. Whether chu-shr, by chance, makes sense or not, many Chinese swear by it.

To the extent that it can be understood, chu-shr feng shui works through three basic techniques:

1. The "connecting ch'i method" ties in ch'i that is too far from a house or too deep beneath the earth's surface. A simple, stopgap variation is to plant into the earth a hollow pole with a light at the top to siphon up the ch'i.

2. The "balancing ch'i method" rounds the environment into harmony with itself and its surroundings. If, for example, a house is awkwardly shaped, a landscape or architectural feature might be added to achieve equilibrium.

3. The "outstanding methods" either increase or modify the flow of ch'i. These can churn and activate weak or stagnant ch'i, circulating it through a house with a bright light, a fountain, or a bubbling fishtank. Strong and dangerous ch'i can be dispersed by moving, musical gizmos such as windmills, wind chimes, and bells.*

---

*Joseph M. Backus, "Lin Yun, Geomancer," *The American Dowser* 19, no. 3 (August 1979), pp. 118–119.

PLOTS OF LAND

Feng shui men consider individual parcels of land. In town areas lack of choice sometimes presents only oddly shaped plots formed by poor planning or natural boundaries such as rivers or hills. In such cases feng shui can balance the asymmetrical angles and give purpose to and enhance awkward shapes.

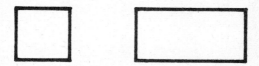

Good plot shapes.

A rectangular or square shape is best. The south side should be open, allowing the sun's rays to enter and warm the house. If the plot is large, the backyard can be a bit higher than the front. But if the garden is small, it is best to have it level rather than sloping. (The latter would let ch'i roll downhill too quickly, like a flood sweeping the family off its feet, taking with it health, social standing, and money.)

In dealing with strange property shapes, Lin Yun says, a feng shui expert must use intuitive talent—strong imagination, common sense, and psychic knowledge—in other words, chu-shr feng shui. "I look at land plots from all angles—whether they are high or low, long or short, square or round—to see what the shape may resemble—be it a fish, animal, or object. Then I add something to activate it into a vital organism pumping good smooth ch'i." In one case, he suggested installing a water fountain to make oddly angled land look like a wind or water wheel, constantly churning and pulsating ch'i. His frequent suggestion for a sloping plot is to balance it with a hollow lamppost, whose light also serves as bait for additional ch'i.

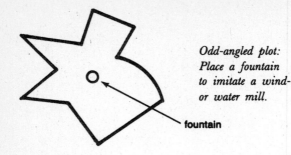

*Odd-angled plot:
Place a fountain
to imitate a wind-
or water mill.*

fountain

Odd plots can sometimes require even odder remedies. In Taipei, for example, five consecutive owners of a squiggly shaped plot lost money and failed in business. The spot, not surprisingly, became widely known for its bad feng shui. The next owners, wanting to open up a restaurant, called in Lin Yun, who made the land represent an auspicious symbol. He advised placing a hollow red pole with a light on it at the narrow end of the plot, with two red poles at the receded entrance, making, among other things, the access wider. And, voilà, it became a scorpion with stinger. (Chinese concepts sometimes differ markedly from Western ideas—bats, for

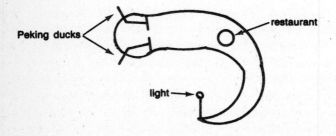

Scorpion-shaped plot for restaurants.

example, are considered lucky. The scorpion is good for a restaurant or a store since it might aggressively pursue its prey, and the owners will thus catch a lot of business.) Lin Yun suggested they continue the metaphor by hanging two Peking ducks—scorpion pincers—outside the entrance. Today the restaurant is a popular Taipei hangout; its owners plan a counterpart in San Francisco.

In another instance, Lin Yun turned a crescent-shaped piece of land into the likeness of a shrimp by advising the owners to install two hollow green lamp poles at the wider end. The family prospered. However, they later painted the poles vibrant red, which

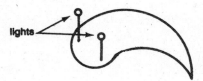

Shrimp-shaped plot: Lights painted red are bad, because red is the color of cooked shrimp. Green lights are good, the color of live shrimp.

under most circumstances signifies good luck to the Chinese, but in this case they lost money. So they called Lin Yun back. He said, in a word, that they were cooked. The problem was the lamppost's red color. "It should be green—red is the color of steamed shrimp." So they painted the lamppost green and all was well.

Even otherwise fine rectangular plots can sometimes have feng shui problems. In Taiwan, for example, a Mr. Chou lived next to a Mr. T'ang, on tracts of land that were virtual mirror images. Mr. Chou one day bought an adjoining plot, lengthening—and unbalancing—his land: It had too much backyard. As his business began to decline, Lin Yun was called in. He suggested a tall, red light post at the long end of the property, and it quickly had the desired effect. When he saw his neighbor's good fortune, Mr. T'ang also installed a similar red lamppost. But, in feng shui, one man's

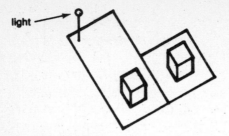

Unbalanced plot:
If plot is too long, balance it with a light.

cure can be another's catastrophe: The T'angs' finances quickly worsened. Explains Lin Yun: "The lamp tilted his property, which originally was balanced."

THE FENG SHUI HOUSE

With the notable exception of Buddhist/Taoist temples, few buildings today go all out to achieve the ancient feng shui ideals. From the ground up, the traditional Chinese house was a universe in itself. Timbers rose from a foundation of stamped soil, symbolically linking heaven and earth. Behind high surrounding walls, a garden court presented all nature in microcosm. And around it, the building itself mimicked the most auspicious feng shui arrangement: the U-shaped, dragon-tortoise-tiger armchair hill, protecting the center and ideally facing south.

The ideal of the garden was both central and simple: No matter how far a house lay from a truly pastoral countryside, its residents must never lose touch with the elemental universe. Nature was made an integral part of the building, just a step away through a courtyard or a glance through a latticework window. Rocks were

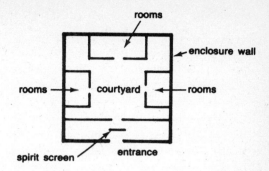

A traditional Chinese compound.

mountains, fish pools were oceans, and bonsai, of course, were old gnarled trees. Against the geometric regularity of a Western garden like Versailles—where man sought to control nature by imposing order on it—Chinese garden courts were irregular, imitating nature in miniature.

The rooms surrounding a garden court embodied the notion "within yin there is yang." Intertwined with Taoist philosophy, the design turned inhabitants away from roads, other people, and the working world toward an ideal of simple nature. (It also supplied both a steady influx of ch'i and excellent ventilation.) The paradox of formal architecture surrounding spontaneous nature was a pleasure rather than a problem. Over the course of thirty centuries, to be sure, elements of out-and-out superstition have crept into Chinese design. Some Chinese saw screens inside of doorways as shields against malign spirits or demons. It was said that demons only flew in straight lines so the screens would repulse them. Often a yin-yang symbol decorated the screen as a protective talisman. An I Ching trigrammed mirror (a ba-gua) might adorn the screen to be placed above the door so that when a demon charged, he would be greeted by his own fierce face, and presumably flee in fear. Painted images such as warlike door gods were hung by the entrance to menace would-be intruders.

The origin of China's traditional sweeping, up-curved roof is unclear. Some say it derives from nomadic tents, others that it mimics a spread of branches or the Chinese character for "tree." Others say it is purely aesthetic. Less scholarly sources insist it is designed to keep devils away. When a devil pounced or fell from the sky, he would slide down the roof and be sent skyward again, and if he fell again, the spiked eaves would impale him. But whatever the explanation, the ornamented roofs also serve a practical purpose: Their eaves allow maximum winter sun to enter, but let in only a minimum of summer sun. (Roofs are more peaked in south China to keep the hot sun out, lower in the north to allow wind to flow over unobstructed.)

Practical concerns were in fact fundamental to much of traditional Chinese design. For thousands of years, the Chinese arranged buildings in such a way as to subject natural forces to human convenience. Aside from carefully calculated roofs, wind screens and masses of earth were used to regulate heat and cold. Ancient palaces had cooling systems with water running down between double walls. And ch'i, of course, was rigorously controlled, using screens, walls, staggered windows, and labyrinthine doors. Even today, many Chinese are uncomfortable with three or more windows or doors lined up on the same axis—the flow of ch'i, they say, is too strong.

Modern House Shapes

Modern architecture and life-styles have, of course, largely ruled out traditional Chinese house design. The task of the modern feng shui man is to create or restore old-style harmony and integrity, normally within a conventional twentieth-century framework. Many layouts are possible, but some are very clearly better than others.

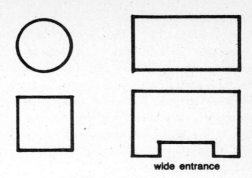

Good house shapes.

As with plots of land, the best house shapes are the most regular: rectangular, square, or even round. A small entrance courtyard, an interior court, or even just a chimney will let ch'i permeate the house. Provided there are no serious problems with the house's location, the result will be a fine structure in which to build solid income and a steady life.

Any of the almost infinite number of odd or irregular shapes can bring trouble. It might be something seemingly innocuous: A

"Small-nosed" house shape: If the front is too small, plant shrubbery or flowers.

small entrance foyer or a "nose" jutting from the house front can choke the influx of ch'i and thus encourage money problems. An arrowlike, sharply angled corner can threaten inhabitants, requiring pools, gardens, or other fixtures to create harmonious balance. On a larger scale, any unbalanced form can cause problems, with various L-shaped or U-shaped arrangements probably the worst offenders.

In ill-shaped houses, placement of the various rooms often decides the occupant's destiny. Feng shui men pay most attention to the location of the master bedroom, where most people spend at

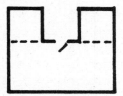

U-shaped house: Place guestroom or gambling room in the wings.

least a third of their lives, and the kitchen, where food is prepared, influencing health and, indirectly, wealth. With a U-shaped house, for example, if the front door is in the concave part with the kitchen behind, then the family, especially the husband, eats out all the time, staying away the entire day. A similarly placed master bedroom would also be a "dangerous situation": The husband will feel like he is sleeping outside, and might in fact end up spending nights elsewhere, symbolically locked outside of the house and family. Other troublesome side effects might include chronic headaches, surgery, failure of careers, frequent changing of jobs, or even getting fired. For such a situation, Lin Yun recommends constructing a screen or wall across the entrance to complete the rectangle and make it seem whole. If the bedroom were instead in one of the wings, making it into a guestroom would at least ensure short visits.

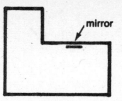

Boot-shaped house: Don't put bedroom on the sole, or hang a mirror to draw it away from the sole.

With the shoelike variety of L-shaped houses, a bedroom along the sole may "trip up" a family's fortune or cause residents to feel "downtrodden," resulting in headaches. Far better is the "ankle area," the juncture for power and energy. For boot-shaped houses, Lin Yun recommends balancing: "On the heel side, plant flowers or vines so the house is never quite stepping down and its weight does not press heavily on the master." This also prevents the entire family from "tripping up" in life. Another solution would be to add a pond, fountain, or artificial river to square off the L, making the house appear complete. With any L-shaped or U-shaped home, the unsettling factors can be modified by placing a mirror within the house to reflect the disconnected wind, thus drawing it into the main part of the building.

Perhaps the most precarious arrangement is a house shaped like a cleaver—doubly so if the bedroom lies against the "blade."

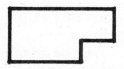

Knife-shaped house: Don't put bedroom on the edge, put it in the handle.

Always "on the edge," an occupant may be exposed to illness—perhaps fatal—or loss of job or money. In such cases, Lin Yun advises moving the bedroom to the handle area, the controlling part and the locus for the power, to become fiercely successful.

Five

URBAN FENG SHUI

In financially and industrially sophisticated Hong Kong, a city which perhaps more than any other devotes itself single-mindedly to the amassing of wealth, people are still having feng shui experts ritually bless and arrange their homes and offices. Feng shui has even infiltrated Westernized sectors of Hong Kong. A real estate ad that ran in an English-language Hong Kong newspaper not only boasted plush, newly built luxury apartments with balconies overlooking the South China Sea and convenient transportation but also promised "excellent feng shui."

To understand urban feng shui, one must first look to the beginnings of a city. Urban feng shui probably grew out of rural practices and became more sophisticated in the hands of imperial court diviners. When they built cities, they considered surrounding natural shapes, orientation, and the auspiciousness of a site.

It was a long process, beginning with divination of a site. In the ancient *Book of Songs,* several poems, including one about the legendary founder of the western Chou dynasty, King Wu, mention observance of feng shui.

> Omens he took, our king,
> Before the building of the capital at Hao:
> The Tortoise directed it:
> King Wu perfected it.
> Oh, glorious King Wu.*

Practical considerations in choosing a site were also important. In one poem describing a first-century A.D. city, good landscape features bring power and good fortune.

> In abundance of flowering plants and fruits
> It is the most fertile of the nine provinces.
> In natural barriers for protection and defense
> It is the most impregnable refuge in heaven and earth.
> This is why its influence has extended in six directions
> This is why it has thrice become the seat of power.†

Once the Chinese chose a site, they set an order on the city's form and hierarchy. Through a symbolic design system, they linked urban planning to other cultural entities: politics, astrology, religion, art. Special attention was paid to capital cities, on the assump-

---

*Arthur Waley, *The Book of Songs* (New York: Grove Press, 1978), p. 264.
†Quoted in Arthur F. Wright, "Symbolism and Function: Reflections on Chang-an and Other Great Cities," *Journal of Asian Studies* (1964), p. 669.

tion that the nation's well-being and the emperor's effectiveness depended on proper alignment with the most potent elements of the universe. So palace and capital layout were patterned after strong natural images and along stellar routes. Because of the emperor's arbitrating position between heaven and earth, the Chinese thought it critical that he sit at the hub, not only of the capital, but also of China—the middle kingdom—and the universe itself. His throne was placed where "earth and sky meet, where the four seasons merge, where wind and rain are gathered in and where yin and yang are in harmony."*

A city's shape is essential to its feng shui. Two forms of urban design arise out of feng shui: One derives power from surrounding natural forms, the other from symbolic shapes.

Hangchow, for instance, China's southern Sung capital, harmonized with the landscape, following the contours of lake and mountain. Reflecting rural influences, its layout responds to natural forces (dangers). Dating back to the Han dynasty (206 B.C.–A.D. 220), Hangchow was a town periodically threatened by floods. Built around a tidal estuary, which became West Lake, the city lay victim to high tides that during equinoxes produce tidal waves. In attempting to rein in the water flow, city governors—among them two renowned poets, Po Chü-i and Su Tung-po—enhanced the scenery's aesthetics and its feng shui with two landscape-gracing dikes.

Symbolic shapes were most prevalent for larger cities. Legend has it that one Ming dynasty plan for Peking's Forbidden City —where the emperor had resided from the twelfth century onward —was human-shaped, with important buildings and halls placed where vital organs should be.

Since the Chou dynasty (1122–256 B.C.) the Chinese have built cities, especially capitals, in square shapes mimicking their image of

---

*Quoted in Roderick MacFarquhar, *The Forbidden City: China's Ancient Capital* (New York: Newsweek, 1978), p. 72.

the earth, which they thought was square. These geometric cities were generally built on a grid of north-south, east-west roads running along a strong central axis. Peking's precise geometric layout struck Marco Polo, the Venetian voyager, as a "chessboard." Centuries before Peking was even a town, the Chinese built Chang-an, the first Chinese capital (c. 200 B.C.), along a north-south axis. Chang-an, modern-day Sian, became a prototype of sorts for later Chinese cities. (In fact, it was designed so auspiciously that the Japanese built two of their ancient capitals, Nara and Kyoto, along the same lines.) During the time of Chang-an, various traditional urban feng shui features were established. To the north lay the market, to the south, the palace. In the center stood the bell tower, which was moved several times as the city grew or shrunk. Government buildings and temples were also auspiciously placed.

Walls were an integral part of a city's feng shui. South of the Great Wall lay many more walls. Thousands of miles of walls surrounded farms, temples, homes, and cities. Both a defense and a definition of the town, walls were built to deter barbarians, harsh winds, and malign spirits. At one point in the Ch'ing dynasty, Westerners petitioned to open Peking's south wall to allow the Peking-Hankow railroad to pass through. The Chinese resisted, claiming Peking was shaped like a dragon: The central south gate was his mouth, the flanking gates his eyes. After the railroad proponents won, the losers warned that the dragon had been wounded and city money (dragon's blood) would seep out.

Mountains were another important feature of urban feng shui. Mountains were huge earth shields that protected the cities from harsh winds and barbarians who swept down from the north. At times mountains were even manufactured. Such was the case of Coal Hill, a 300-foot-high artificial mountain directly north of Peking. Coal Hill's origins can be traced to the thirteenth century, around the time the Mongol chieftain Genghis Khan was born. Chinese geomancers predicted that a hill to the north possessed a "king-making vital force" that would ultimately destroy them. Attempting to forestall this threat, they lavished gifts on the northern Mongols in return for their allowing the Chinese to tear down the hill and move its earth south to Peking, where they piled up the new hill. Shortly after the Chinese completed this huge endeavor, wasting men and money, the Mongols attacked, setting up their own capital and dynasty.

These mountain screens, obviously deriving from rural rules of orientation, reflect a near-obsessive Chinese aversion to the north. The emperor resided in Peking, sitting on his dragon throne with his back to the north, shielding China from the myriad evils emitted from the north. By facing south he also benefited from sun and sea, while governing over his kingdom. Not only was this position good for the emperor personally but it was also auspicious for China. (Because of the south-facing of China's rulers, all maps were drawn opposite to ours, placing the south at the top and the north at the bottom.)

In siting a city or town, the Chinese generally avoided flat, featureless plains where winds and floods could whip through streets. When the British, French, and German "foreign devils" encroached on Chinese soil and demanded trading outposts, the Chinese emperor and governors bowed, giving with perhaps a slight smirk the low sections of Shanghai, Tientsin, and Hankow, not incidentally with the worst feng shui and riddled with malign spirits. (The foreigners, to the amazement of the Chinese, improved the settlement area's flat feng shui by constructing tall, mountainlike buildings.)

Hong Kong Island itself was spurned by the Chinese. In 1842, after the first Opium War, they ceded it to the British, figuring that with its bad feng shui, it was sort of a Trojan horse. Devoid of beneficial ch'i and plagued by pirates, it was called the "barren rock." The British initially encountered problems in developing the island, and instead of improving the feng shui, they made it even worse. They began building the first commercial trading center in a low area, ironically named "Happy Valley," a mile away from the ports. To create their business center, they built roads that the Chinese claimed maimed the guardian dragon by severing his feet. The British leveled hills and filled in lakes, thus wiping out chances for financial opportunity. The resulting low swampland became a breeding ground for malaria-carrying mosquitoes. After several people became ill and died, the Chinese workers boycotted the development as bad feng shui, and the trading center was more auspiciously relocated in Hong Kong central, where it thrives today, backed by mountains and looking out on water.

CITY LIFE

Today some town feng shui principles can be and have been applied, if unwittingly, to certain city-planning concepts. Parks, no matter how small, and tree-lined streets bring ch'i and its beneficial effects to local residents. Apartments or offices with river views, gardens or balconies, and space or southern exposure are also good. (In Peking, the rent for apartments with southern exposure is a third higher than those facing the north.)

When Lin Yun visited New York City in 1978, one civic-minded friend took him up in a helicopter to check out the city's ch'i. His insights were not surprising. Those living around Central Park with its grass, trees, and reservoir enjoy the best ch'i, while those living on Roosevelt Island—"a barren, featureless rock surrounded by too much water"—have the worst. He said that the amount of ch'i penetrating the island's rocky terrain was so small that the Roosevelt Islanders might be hard-pressed to retain their jobs or positions, much less succeeed professionally. He added that while the Midtown area is good, the United Nations' ch'i suffers under the oppressive influences of the towering Citicorp building, making the international organization sluggish in acting on important issues.

Naturally, urban ch'i differs from town ch'i and even more from country ch'i. Lin Yun explains:

In the country, life is more stable and calm. But remember, good feng shui in the country depends on good earth ch'i: If ch'i is good, life will be smooth, prosperous, and happy. If ch'i is lacking, life will be more troublesome. Ch'i fluctuates more in the city than in the country. It can be particularly good, or exceptionally bad—there is a greater potential for unusual occurrences, such as making a million dollars a month or losing it, or falling prey to senseless, extreme violence. The variation of people's fates and fortune is greater.

Even if a city's ch'i is good, many things can alter it. An area endowed with excellent, balanced ch'i doesn't necessarily make for good feng shui: Corners, roads, buildings, or other construction works might destroy the harmony. Because of this, city planning and awareness of the urban environment are important.

The site of a tree, the bend in a river, or the shape of a hill, however, often makes little difference. The overall urban environment is determined not so much by natural landscape features as by man-made structures. In the cityscape, high buildings replace mountains, roads are scrutinized as rivers once were. So the urban geomancer pays attention to the size, shape, and even color of skyscrapers, the direction and turns of overpasses and roads, and the angle of a building's corner.

Street patterns, for example, play a greater role in urban feng shui. A house above the confluence of roads is fine. Living below, however, where the streets seem to point like arrows, can be as dangerous as living at the point of a knifelike road. Increased traffic—cars racing down knifelike urban roads—is particularly lethal and disruptive, dispersing harmonious ch'i. The occupant of a building facing oncoming traffic may not only be a victim of continuous stabs from strong, killing ch'i and fierce winds, but may also be bombarded with the sounds of car horns and motors and the sharp screeches of tires.

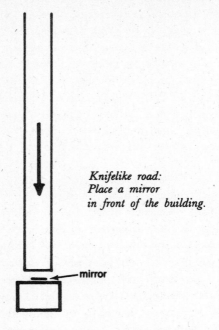

Knifelike road:
Place a mirror
in front of the building.

mirror

The proliferation of gambling, drugs, and prostitution in one Kowloon building was blamed not on poor law enforcement but on bad feng shui—the roads joining together in an arrowhead pattern gave it a deadly atmosphere. The repercussions are often serious. One Hong Kong businessman explains: "It's proven to me. It's bad to have an apartment facing oncoming traffic. One friend moved into one such flat. Six months later his girl friend died. After another six months he was fired. It affects your physionometry."

The shape and position of government buildings are still credited with a country's or city's harmony. Chinese still base Hong Kong's successes and failures on the siting of government buildings

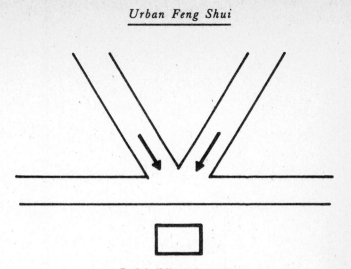

Bad building placement.

and land shapes. They trace the colony's financial success to the correct position of the governor's mansion. On the other hand, they blame Hong Kong's high crime rate on the fact that the central courthouse sits on a good site, thus encouraging crime to thrive. One planner in the Hong Kong government suggests that a further blow to the colony's law and order fell from a knifelike airport runway built out into the harbor. Arriving jets continually stab the belly of one of Kowloon's nine protective dragons. A remedy, he proposes, might be to disguise the saber strip by filling in the harbor on either side of the runway.

The Chinese use feng shui to interpret the destinies of other countries. Looking out from the Washington Monument, Lin Yun noted that some American presidents' problems and tragedies of the country itself could be traced to the siting of the White House. A president must reside in an auspicious place both for the country to be strong, rich, and lucky and for the man himself to be a wise leader. On one hand, the president enjoys good feng shui from the strong curves of the Ellipse and the White House lawn in back of the

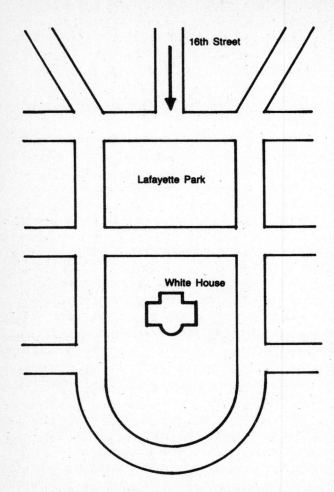

Knifelike road: aerial view of the White House.

executive mansion. These lawn formations, he notes, represent the nation as a whole unit full of smooth-flowing ch'i. (An ellipse evokes the wholeness, the coming together of opposites of the symbol *tao*.) The problems, says Lin Yun, stem from the arrowlike quality of 16th Street, which shoots "killing" ch'i right to the heart of the executive mansion's entrance. The straight road's impact, he says, causes divisiveness in the nation and blasts away the area's positive or smooth ch'i, so that the president cannot govern to his fullest potential.

The cure for the White House's disruptive avenue, says Lin Yun, would be to install a water fountain or windmill to disperse the strong ch'i, making it spread out, like positive ripples, throughout Washington. Monuments, such as the Lincoln and Jefferson memorials, are, in general, good feng shui, helping a nation's luck by bringing up earth ch'i. Monuments, however, can also portend the country's future. When he looked up at the Washington Monument from outside, Lin Yun commented on the two shades of the obelisk, as if it were a national thermometer registering and forecasting the country's future. He interpreted Washington's ch'i by reading the monument. The lighter shade at the bottom third of the stone needle indicates a strong, healthy ch'i, he said—with perhaps more hindsight than foresight—meaning rapid development, prosperity, and power for the United States. But the ch'i, or light shade, rises only so far and then stops. He said that the United States had recently hit a leveling-off period, the dividing line of lighter and darker shades. For several more years the country will seem to be slumping, almost sliding back, in all fields—military, economic, scientific. The United States will eventually forge ahead again, but it will never progress at the velocity of its earlier years.

Lin Yun says Washington's ch'i is losing its vitality. The capital needs something to attract and activate good ch'i again. Lin Yun suggests using a chu-shr method—constructing a heavy monument or building somewhere around the Ellipse or slightly outside Washington city lines. Another, more simple method, he says, would be installing a large bright light in that area to create and attract ch'i.

The significance of the placement of a government building extends even to a city capital. During a New York City mayoral campaign in 1977, a Vietnamese geomancer was asked which candidate would win. On checking out City Hall's alignment, he said it really didn't matter—the building's feng shui was so miserable that whoever won would have to face an overwhelming assortment of feng shui problems. It was a no-win situation.

BUILDING DESIGN

Many urban feng shui problems come from the shapes, heights, and juxtaposition of nearby buildings and structures. In city feng shui, the earth seems ignored to the point of being abused. Indeed, earth dragons are trampled and suffocated by the weight of high buildings and then skewered by their knifelike shapes, while arrowlike roads puncture their flesh. Water dragons are diverted or dammed up. So the design of buildings is crucial.

In Hong Kong, people point to the ultramodern Connaught Center, which houses a lot of foreign companies, as a prime example of faulty feng shui. As local Chinese watched the circular-windowed building rise fifty-two stories above Hong Kong's waterfront, they nicknamed it "Sing Chin Ko Szee Fat Long," "the House of a Thousand Assholes," ostensibly for the porthole shape of its windows, but also, some suspect, for its tenants. The $80 million highrise's problems didn't end at name-calling: Expensive Italian tiles started falling off its outer walls; water main breaks caused four successive floods; and elevators began blitzing out, sometimes trapping their riders, sometimes plummeting several stories past their destinations—leading some Western bankers to dub the building "Hancock East" after the problem-plagued John Hancock Insurance Building in Boston, Massachusetts.*

Call it what you may, the Chinese trace the Connaught Center's unforeseen structural problems not to poor cement or bad engineering, but to feng shui, saying it lacks ritual balancing of the natural elements. They criticize the contractor's disregard of the winds, water, and the placement and design of the building.

Several explanations tend toward the graphically death-oriented, such as: The round windows apparently resemble the circular photographs of the deceased on Chinese tombstones; the headstonelike building is aligned with the Peak Tower restaurant, which looks like the urn in which incense sticks are burned as an offering for the dead. Some occupants conveniently blame their financial woes on the fact that the building looks like a crab cage pulled out of the harbor, with water—symbolizing money—pouring out of the holes.

The Chinese see a direct relationship between the symbol of

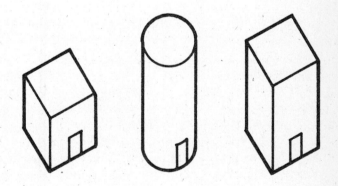

Good building shapes.

*Veronica Huang, "Hong Kong's Tower of Assorted Trouble," *Wall Street Journal,* October 12, 1976, p. 1; and Roy Rowan, *Fortune* (October 1977), p. 191.

their buildings' shapes and the destinies, welfare, and behavior of their occupants, much as Chinese in the country say mountains shape their lives and fortunes. Uncomplicated square-shaped, cylindrical, and rectangular buildings are fine. Some shapes can be downright auspicious. The Hong Kong/USA Asian Trade Center in Oakland, California, is a consortium of octagonal buildings imitating the ba-gua symbol of the *I Ching*. The project, drawing from the mystical resources of the *I Ching*, is totally eight-sided—skylight, tiles, fountain, flowerpots, benches, kiosks, towers.

This idea draws precedent from early Chinese architecture. The Temple of Heaven, south of Peking, where the emperor annually sacrificed animals to heaven, was built in a propitious shape. Leaving the square (earth) plaza, the emperor mounted round (heaven) steps, auspiciously numbered in multiples of three and nine, to pray for a lucky year, good harvest, and reaffirmation of the Mandate of Heaven, his divine right to rule.

The most potent fear, an old feng shui carry-over, is death-oriented symbolism. In Hong Kong, modern housing complexes glisten with woks and mirrors that residents place outside their windows to ward off the bad luck of church crosses. A Chinese minister explained: "They think it is the cross of death and we believe it is the cross of love."

This philosophy was the bane of Western missionaries in China. In the nineteenth century, the missionary-scholar Reverend Edkins described feng shui as "one of the great obstacles to the progress of civilization," which, he wrote, "checks the efforts of missionary zeal." In the nineteenth century, missionaries were forced to remove the earth-impaling crosses from their churches. But the Chinese didn't single out Christians, insisting Moslems also remove minarets from their mosques.

Throughout Asia, the Chinese avoid living directly across from a church or a Buddhist temple. One family living across from a church in Hong Kong fell ill—a liver problem, a strange high fever, and so on. The dread cause was the coffin-shaped hexagonal church windows.

Other fears evoked by churches range from the overbearing, formalized religious architecture to the harmful draw and power of the building, which, the Chinese insist, can drain good ch'i from a building it faces. Even in New York City, the Chinese will board up windows and change entrances to thwart the draining of·ch'i from their offices toward a church.

Because of the strong association of funeral parlors with death, most Chinese avoid living or working near them. But with the lack of space and choice in a city, often commercial and residential sectors must mingle. This can be disturbing if you happen to live across from a funeral parlor. The rental rates of an apartment house went down when a funeral home went up beside it. Said one tenant, "No one likes to be reminded of the dead."

Feng shui symbolism often reflects the actual potential of a design. In Mei Foo Sun Chuen, a large housing estate in the New Territories, some of the tens of thousands of residents interpreted a nearby incinerator as portending death. They said it would hurt local feng shui because its three 100-foot-high chimneys rose like incense stacks, billowing smoke and ash, making their own buildings resemble tombstones. In this case, the symbol imitated the detrimental potential outcome of the incinerator's pollution.

The heights of surrounding buildings, no matter what shape, can oppress an apartment's ch'i, hampering personal and financial growth. The occupant will constantly feel overshadowed and overwhelmed. A Hong Kong businessman explains: "My own factory business wasn't doing well, because a cinema towered over and oppressed it, so we hung a mirror and business improved until we had a bad month again. I looked up one day and noticed the mirror was broken. So we replaced it and now things are going well again."

Another case is the apartment of Lin Ke-fan, a violinist. When Mr. Lin arrived in Hong Kong from China, he could afford only an apartment reputed to have bad feng shui. Soon his luck soured, his money ran out, and his work failed. He called in Lin Yun, who divined that the problem lay in the juxtaposition of Mr. Lin's second-floor walk-up surrounded by highrises.

The skyscrapers apparently oppressed Mr. Lin's ch'i, not allowing him to perform to his full capabilities. All this was changed by the simple expedient of hanging a red hexagonal mirror outside one window. The mirror, bordered with the I Ching trigrams, blocked the overbearing qualities of taller buildings and reflected them back. This, however, raised a perennial feng shui problem: The tactics that benefit one person may be the demise of another. One nearby family developed sudden, inexplicable illnesses, and to appease his desperate neighbors, Mr. Lin removed the mirror from outside. (Unknown to the family, the mirror hangs inside, still facing in their direction.)

Besides the hexagonal mirror, another effective panacea for a building's inferior height is to place a pool of water on the roof. Lin Yun says this works particularly well not only because it reflects the taller structures' oppressiveness back at the buildings but also because the images mirrored in the water are standing horizontally, as if they have collapsed. The pool also allows ch'i to circulate and rise in the building.

Another good distortion of a Goliath-size building is the convex mirror, reflecting the perpetrating highrise upside-down.

A building's symbolism can affect the lives and business of its tenants. Knife-shaped and boot-shaped buildings are to be avoided. In Singapore, some businessmen link the failure of a modern shopping mall to its coffin shape. Feng shui men initially vetoed the plan but it was built anyway; now the shopping center is commercially dead, a self-perpetuating prophecy.

If an apartment building has towers that give it the shape of a meat cleaver, the occupant may be eating, sleeping, and working on the edge. Living in the tower, the handle of the knife, on the other hand, can improve the residents' ch'i, giving them a sense of con-

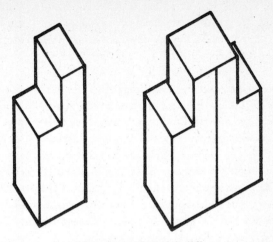

Meat-cleaver-shaped buildings.

trol. A mirror hung on the wall opposite the edge wall will bring the occupant and his/her desk, bed, or table away from the blade to safety.

Chinese residents of Hong Kong refused to buy apartments in two tall, luxury harborside towers. A cloudy future, they said, stems from flashing red lights on top of the buildings to warn away planes: At night, the buildings look like lighted offertory candles or incense sticks used at funerals or in ancestral shrines. Many Westerners embrace this way of thinking because cries of bad feng shui lower the high rent and occupancy rates; thus, they lease these luxury apartments for considerably less money than normal.

Urban feng shui adepts consider not only where to live, but how high. Lin Yun, applying principles similar to those of town placement on a mountain, says an apartment dweller must find a balance—living not too high or too low—somewhere between Scylla and Charybdis. Living on the top floors isn't the most stable situation. Although the view may be expansive, strong winds disperse ch'i, buffet the building, and rattle windows. A very tall building can also sway a bit with the wind.

The lower floors, on the other hand, are oppressed by the height of other buildings and the weight of higher floors. Less sunlight gets in. They are also more susceptible to the bad influences of traffic, pollution, and street noises.

A building's entrance is important. It should be wide enough to let in a healthy stream of ch'i. It should not directly face trees or columns, both of which obstruct ch'i from entering as well as oppressing the ch'i of those exiting the building. In the initial design for the multimillion-dollar Hong Kong/USA Asian Trade Center in Oakland, California, a Texas architect had a support column blocking the main entrance to the complex. Explains one employee of Gammon Properties, Ltd., a Hong Kong real estate concern: "The architect paid little attention to feng shui. When the boss saw the column in front of the main door, he said, 'This won't do at all.'" So they moved the entrance, and knocked out a new one unhindered by a pillar. A rounded pillar, however, won't hurt the occupants as much as a square one, because ch'i can move smoothly around it, and no corners jut out to harm it.

Businesses follow their own feng shui rules. It is best to have a store sited where the ch'i can easily enter. Applying rural river concepts, a store at the confluence of roads will get a steady stream of business and money. An American banker at Hong Kong Citibank joked that much of the success of the international banking concern in the region came from the building resting right where several roads meet. A store in the middle of a long arrowlike thoroughfare will not fare as well. As Tao Ho, a Harvard-trained architect, says:

> As an architect, when I talk about environmental design, in fact I am talking about good feng shui. . . . A shop at a corner has very good feng shui, because a lot of people are walking from different sides and also because of the stoplight. You take away the stoplight and people must rush across the street ignor-

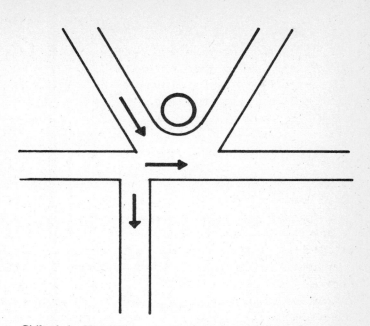

Citibank in Hong Kong: An example of good building placement.

ing the shop. If the light is red every few seconds, people will stop and buy. If there isn't a light, business won't be so good, people won't stop. There's a lot of sense to feng shui and that's what today is called planning to human needs.

Often the Chinese make a corner shop, hotel, or bank entrance slanted so that access to business is widened and ch'i, people, and money are all drawn in. For years these slanted doors were used mostly by gambling operations, as they still are in Macao's casinos. When a Hong Kong bank opened a branch with a slanted entrance a few years ago, many Chinese were alarmed at the symbolic allusion to the way the bank might be actually handling their money—cutting corners to make cash.

———

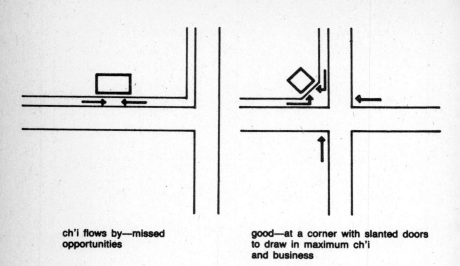

ch'i flows by—missed
opportunities

good—at a corner with slanted doors
to draw in maximum ch'i
and business

Store sites.

The slanted door's financial benefits are derived from the door's relationship to the street. Good ch'i, and therefore money, will be drawn in, affecting the ch'i of the other cross streets so they, too, are directed toward the door. When Lin Yun did the feng shui of Ywe Hwa, a large store selling only products from the People's Republic of China, Lin Yun suggested they install slanted doors at a corner for an entrance—and business is booming. Indeed, the slanted door allows greater access to the bank or store, making entrance easier for more people from a variety of directions. The slanted door not only blunts what might have been a sharp corner but also creates part of a ba-gua symbol, adding even more auspiciousness to the door formation.

Water is an important element in making money. In business, the Chinese say, it is so important to the feng shui of the Hong Kong and Shanghai Bank that the institution gave the colonial government money to build a park and a low-lying garage so that its view of Victoria Harbor—or access to water—would not be interrupted. Lin Yun says that when water bodies are not available, outdoor fountains are good, simultaneously bringing up good ch'i. Pointing to a large fountain in Hong Kong's Sha Tin racecourse, Lin Yun once said that it was good for the raceway's business, bringing money back to the track, ensuring that people will return another day.

The Chinese use the words *feng shui* as slang for gambling. According to Lin Yun, the presence of ocean water on the Atlantic City shore presents ''a lot of opportunity to make money.'' But because the water is less than pristinely clear, not surprisingly, ''the chance of intrigue exists.''

While villagelike claims of feng shui incursions and subsequent extortion seldom happen, some bogus feng shui claims arise from a face-saving mechanism. According to an American lawyer in Hong Kong, one elderly Chinese businessman used feng shui to save his sons' face. The sons had drawn up a contract to buy a large hotel in the southwestern United States. Seeing that his sons had made a mistake and the hotel wasn't worth the price, the old man complained that the building in question lacked the correct balance of wind and water and that under such circumstances, he would not buy the hotel—thus extricating his money and his sons' honor from a foolish business deal.

Stories of feng shui deception abound in Hong Kong. According to Hong Kong legend, in the 1930s a feng shui priest warned a Mr. Eu that he would live as long as he built houses. So for years Mr. Eu added castlelike wings and turrets onto his already sprawling mansions; there were three in all—Euston, Eucliff, and Sermio. When the Japanese invaded in 1941, building stoppped and Mr. Eu—as prophesied—died shortly thereafter. Some Hong Kong residents say the feng shui man and the architect were in league.

Some people, on the other hand, go so far as to equate their well-earned prosperity with good feng shui. No matter how wealthy they are and how many mansions they may own, their official address will remain in a run-down section of Hong Kong where they first made their fortune. They see themselves not so much as self-made but as men whose money was destined to come to them because of their auspicious home or office. They keep the house as we might keep a rabbit's paw. The theory is: as long as his official address is this place where he got his start, then good luck will follow him.

One amah will not allow her employers, the Edgars, to move, saying their Hong Kong apartment brought them eleven relatively lucky years—no ill occurrences, no bad health. But, more important, the Edgars' mid-level home is *her* "good luck" flat. "Our luck is OK," says Sylvia Edgar, "but everything our amah does turns out well; she'll buy land in Lan Tao and the property costs will double. Everything she touches turns to gold. Although she has property and land, and is probably wealthier than we are, she likes living in our flat. She says it gives her luck and if luck is what she has, she has a lot of it."

Six

INTERIORS: ARCHITECTURE

Apartments and offices have the greatest impact on city dwellers. The inside is the base of a city person's life, determining and shaping ch'i. Interiors with good feng shui nourish the residents' ch'i, so they will both thrive in the outside world and handle hostile circumstances ranging from gun-point robberies to cutting tongues. On the other hand, to live in an ill-designed interior is asking for trouble. Bad feng shui hampers the occupants' potential, causing stress, irritability, and, ultimately, unhappiness. If the inside is not balanced, a good neighborhood will be of little help. According to

Lin Yun, "If people live and work in surroundings that harm or stunt their own ch'i, nothing will succeed. Other places will develop, but an area with unbalanced residents will degenerate." Thus, in cities, modern feng shui men stress inside ch'i.

Although the country generally offers better ch'i, a city dweller can remedy urban ills—lack of space, sunlight, trees, and water—by using feng shui antidotes and thus control his or her environment. Nevertheless, interior rules also apply to rural and suburban homes.

Lin Yun uses chu-shr methods to give meaning to spaces and to activate ch'i; to resolve hostile surroundings; to balance unharmonious habitats; to channel the energy in rooms to improve occupants' energy and thus their performance in the world. Feng shui staples include mirrors, lighting, symbolism, wind chimes, and plants.

A house resembles a body because it has its own metabolism. Ch'i must flow evenly throughout, pumping smoothly from hall to room. Windows and doors, the house's "noses" and "mouths," separate inside ch'i from outside ch'i. Once inhaled, ch'i is ideally channeled from space to space by doors, walls, screens, halls, corners, plants, and furniture. The occupants, a house's vital organs, are nourished by a healthy, balance flow of ch'i—not too strong and not too weak—to operate to their fullest capacity.

The door size, for example, should be balanced with the house. A proportionately small entrance is like having a tiny mouth: It doesn't allow enough ch'i to get in to circulate, thus diminishing chances of health, wealth, and happiness. On the other hand, if the door is too large, too much ch'i will enter. To remedy a small door, place a mirror on the top or on the sides of the door to give the effect of height and width. If the door is too large, install a wind chime in the front hall to disperse harmfully strong ch'i currents.

DOORS: ENTRANCES

Good feng shui often depends on entrance doors' shape, size, and orientation. If the front door's feng shui is wrong, disaster may befall the household. Because of this, some people enter only through their back doors. A famous Hong Kong actress walks through the servants' quarters to enter her elegant apartment. A Chinese housewife living in Shek-O, a posh section of Hong Kong island, was told that all good things were going out of her front door, so she blocked it off despite protests from her European husband. Nonetheless, everybody from servants to guests entered through the back door. And their luck changed—so much so that when the husband later moved his offices, he called in a feng shui man who told him he needed two doors. After making the necessary adjustments, he fared very well.

The entrance sets the tone, the "vibes," of a house. As Lin Yun says, "If you are sensitive enough when you enter a house, you have various feelings—some give you a happy feeling, some make you uncomfortable and depressed." Traditionally hospitable, the Chinese arrange an entrance, the protection from the outside and the threshold into an inner world, more for the resident's benefit than for the visitor's. A faulty entrance barely affects the visitor. But to the resident it is one of many house features that can mold or program ch'i. If ch'i is continually sparse or withdrawn, then residents will become more timid, almost self-destructive. Their ch'i will retreat and their movements will be reserved. If ch'i is balanced and flows smoothly, on the other hand, residents will prosper. Thus, light and dark, distance and nearness, solid and space must be complementary, a balanced base from which to embark on a successful life course.

The ideal is to walk into a wide, light room or lobby with an expansive, happy feeling. This will encourage residents' minds, movements, and emotions to be expressive, unburdened, and constructive. Make sure doors open to the broadest area of an apart-

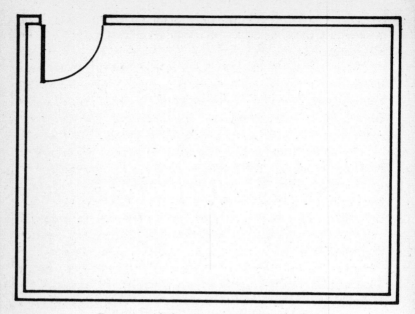

Entrances: ideal entrance—maximum view.

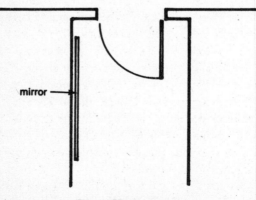

mirror

George Hsu's entrance.

ment or room for maximum view of the interior. Some Hong Kong businessmen have had the hinges of all their office doors reversed for this reason.

There should be no obstacles to ch'i. A lobby or an entrance hall can affect both the building and the occupant. If the hall or lobby is too narrow, ch'i can only trickle into the house, causing health and development problems. Like an undersized windpipe, it will suffocate the tenants' luck and choke their careers.

Take, for example, the foyer of the residence of George Hsu, the Hong Kong representative for General Electric. On entering the apartment, the Hsus were first greeted by a narrow, dark tunnel of a hallway punctuated by a beam that hovered low, further obstructing ch'i. This, claims Mr. Hsu, caused his children to be constantly ill, and, ultimately, his wife to die in childbirth. Distraught, he sought feng shui advice. To widen the narrow foyer, he placed a wide mirror on the hall wall visible from the entrance, thus adding apparent depth and allowing ch'i to expand through the obstructing wall. Mr. Hsu then installed a false translucent glass ceiling lit by overhead lights, thus obscuring the beam and encouraging his ch'i to rise toward the light.

Similarly, a wall directly in front of the entrance also can confine ch'i, making the occupant feel defeated, as if he were constantly coming up against a literal brick wall.

The solution to confined entrances, whether to a room, a hall, an apartment, or an office, is to hang a mirror on the offending wall, extending the visual area so the wall does not obstruct the movement of ch'i. For an oppressive wall parallel to the door, hang an appealing picture or poster of, say, a landscape to draw forward the person's ch'i. A bright light in the hall will draw up and expand ch'i. When the bulb goes out, replace it with an equally bright or even brighter light, never a dimmer one.

Ch'i that flows too strongly can inhibit residents' ch'i. To modify ch'i flow, the Chinese traditionally avoid having three or more doors or windows in a row. This arrangement—reminiscent of

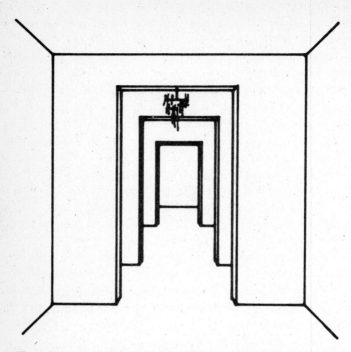

Three doors or windows in a row: Hang a wind chime or mobile to disperse ch'i.

arrowlike rivers and roads—funnels ch'i too quickly. It can cut the house in two, causing differing opinions within the household. A draft, itself a subtle physical barrier, can cause subconscious emotional walls affecting family relationships. The draft's invisible force can also carry away money and threaten family members with possible surgical operations deriving mostly from internal problems along the center vertical line of the body.

The Chinese traditionally place a screen between the doors to fend off strong ch'i and to thwart demons, who tend to fly in straight lines. Another antidote to domestic divisiveness is to have all bedrooms on one side of the hall. This, however, is a bit risky, subjecting the family to extreme changes in fortune that can be sometimes good, sometimes disastrous. The best overall cure is to hang a wind chime, a mobile, or a beaded curtain in the door's line of fire to disperse the strong ch'i current evenly throughout the house.

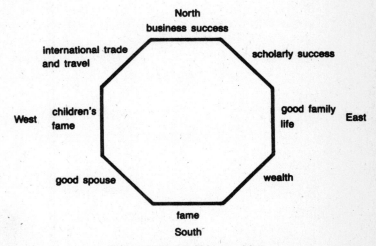

Bed and door I-Ching positions.

Unused or "dead" doors can also cause internal bickering. They inhibit the current of ch'i. A mirror hung on a "dead" door will cure the situation and give apparent depth to the door.

A door's orientation can help determine destiny. One orientation method is based on the octagonal I Ching symbol: Doors facing any of the eight possible directions bestow different fortunes. A door to the north brings good business, to the south means fame, to the east brings good family life, and facing the west bestows fame on offspring. A door facing northeast means scholarly success and intelligence, to the northwest promises family members will travel far and develop interests outside the home, to the southeast means wealth, and to the southwest a good spouse.

Door Alignment

Door alignment is crucial. Doors should face each other directly, and should not overlap. (Two bathroom doors, however, should not face each other.) Overlapping but parallel doors should be avoided. A potentially harmful door arrangement is when two doors are centered along the same axis, but one door is larger than another. This alignment is fine if the big door opens onto a large room, such as a bedroom, living room, or guestroom. The small

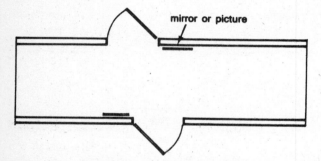

Door alignments: Overlapping parallel doors and different size doors on same axis.

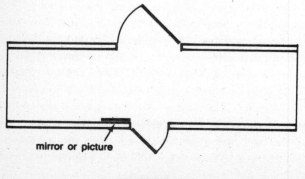

door should open to a small room—a closet, a kitchen, or a bathroom. Because large overpowers small, a large door opening onto a bathroom can cause health and personality problems—big doors should lead to big things. If it opens onto a bathroom, then the residents will always be there, either sick from indigestion or vainly preparing their faces. Hang a mirror or pretty picture outside the large door to draw residents out. Also to be avoided is having two doorknobs knock together when the doors are opened, causing family arguments. Either rehinge the door or paint small red dots at eye level on each door.

Worst of all is when two doors are slightly out of alignment, though not apparent to the eye. This can harm health, career, and family peace. Imitating a bad bite, two family members will always

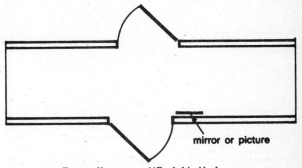

mirror or picture

Door alignment: "Bad bite" doors.

be at odds, arguing and differing in opinions. This "bad-bite" door alignment can unbalance residents' ch'i with its knifelike corner. It also presents an uneven vista. If a person is constantly confronted with two views—one quickly ending at a wall and the other looking long-range into the next room—his or her body's inner harmony and ch'i flow can be disturbed. The situation is similar to wearing eyeglasses with the wrong prescription; the wearer will feel disassociated and unfocused with and without the glasses.

Antidote to uneven doors: Either hang a mirror to give the impression of extended space on the nearer wall, or place something attractive on the wall, something pleasing to the occupant. For example, a picture of a favorite child on the wall will direct attention and ch'i toward the child. A businessman might mount a $100 bill. So the occupants' perspective on life and the world will be balanced, directed, and in focus.

Slanted Doors

The most dangerous door is the slanted door—one on a bias or under a slanted ceiling. A slanted door can destroy good feng shui, bringing on an unusually horrible, unimaginable occurrence.

Slanted walls, beams, or doors can cause fluky catastrophes. Take the case of the family living under a slanted beam: Their child went out to the airport to join his classmates flying to England where they studied. While all his friends were on time to board the jet, he arrived too late and flew on the next plane, which crashed. Although the child survived, his hand was badly injured. Explains Lin Yun, "If you have something slanted, something slanted—oblique, warped, unimaginable—will occur. For example, if I work hard in business, I should be quite successful, but the outcome will be different. Someone less dedicated will get ahead."

To straighten a slanted beam, door, or wall, either hang from the beam, door, or wall a pretty awninglike curtain edged with small silk tassels or add wood, flowers, or plants. Another method is to build a complementary slant on the thinner side of the beam, to fashion a ba-gua symbol.

WINDOWS

The window's shape and style can determine ch'i flow. It is best to install a window that opens completely—outwardly or inwardly—

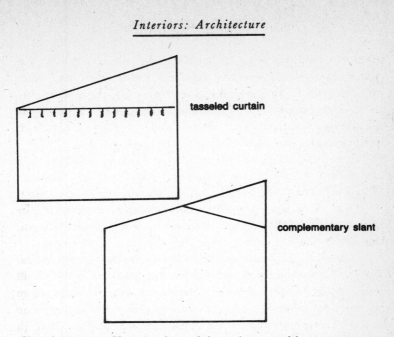

Slanted structures: Hang a red, tasseled curtain or wood beam to even out slant, or build a complementary slant.

instead of one that slides up or down. An outward-opening window is best. It enhances the occupant's ch'i and career opportunities because the maximum amount of ch'i can enter and circulate inside. The movement of opening stretches the occupant's ch'i outward. Some inward-opening windows, on the other hand, can hurt ch'i and thus careers. No obstacles should be in the way to interfere with the ch'i flow and the flow of the opening process.

If a window opens halfway, as do many in old New England homes, this causes the resident to give a false impression to others, because they get only half the ch'i.

Chinese sometimes spurn a good view, blocking off windows for feng shui reasons. Usually, that window looks to the west, the source of oppressive late afternoon sun glare, which can interrupt work and bring on headaches.

At the American Chamber of Commerce in Hong Kong, a certain seat seemed to be a chair of death for all its occupants. When two consecutive employees who sat there died, the editor of its newsletter, June Shaplen, hired a feng shui man who suggested that malign forces were entering through a west window. After blinds were hung and kept shut in the afternoon, all went well.

In Eric Cumine's architectural office, western windows were also blocked off to shield his office from the outside road. According to Mr. Cumine, "The stream of traffic takes money away." Some people board up windows to fence out the bad ch'i emanating from churches and temples. Others draw blinds on nearby brothels and sailor bars.

A window's size and juxtaposition with interior doors is important in determining the house's inner flow of ch'i. Family accord hinges on the relative size and number of doors and windows. More specifically, the window-door relationship is like that of child and parent—the relationship between generations. The door (parent's mouth) must be more impressive than the window (child's mouth) or else the children will be rebellious.

The ratio of windows to doors also affects family harmony. While one window is fine, three or more can lead to family arguments—too many tongues lead to too many options. Too many windows mean that sons and daughters will criticize and argue with and even talk back to their parents. Family unrest can also occur if the window is larger, because the child won't listen to the parents. It is fine, however, to have a large window with smaller sections or panes.

The cure is to put a bell or wind chime on top of the door or where an opening door can ring it. The window (child) may be so big it won't mind the door, but when the door opens and constantly makes a sound, the window must pay attention.

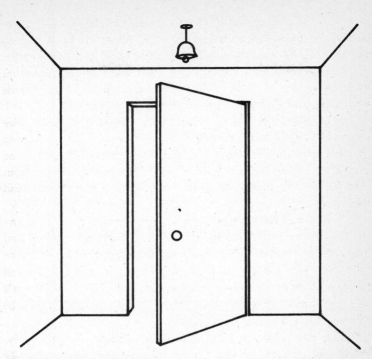

Door-window ratio: If windows outnumber doors 3 to 1, or if the window is larger than the door, hang a bell or wind chime so the door rings the wind chime when it opens.

BEAMS AND PROJECTIONS

Low-lying beams and rafters, burdens to prosperity and growth, should be avoided. Beams not only oppress the ch'i of those underneath them, but also impede ch'i circulation throughout the house. Although exposed rafters in Western homes and beams held together with exquisite joinery in Chinese temples and pavilions are an attractive addition to any building, the Chinese consider beams—especially the central support—dangerous.

Debilitating if situated above an entrance, a bed, a dining table, or a stove, beams oppress ch'i. By supporting the weight of the house, beams emit an overbearing and unnerving pressure on those directly underneath. A beam above the entrance will cause a sort of psychic compression that thwarts not only business and career hope, but also personal development.

The harm caused by beams in a bedroom varies with their position. A rafter above the head of a bed may be the source of constant headaches. Above the stomach, a beam can cause ulcers, backaches, and indigestion. Above the feet, beams can make the occupant immobile, unable to travel or act on anything.

A rafter above the dining table will ensure that lent money will never be returned and that subsequently the occupant will lose

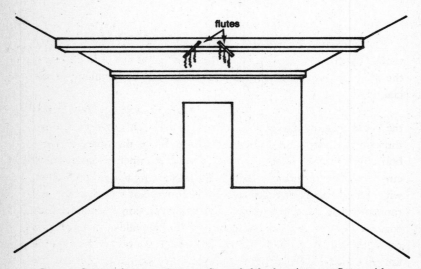

Beams: Create a ba-gua *(octagonal) symbol by hanging two flutes with tassels. The flutes pump ch'i through oppressive beams.*

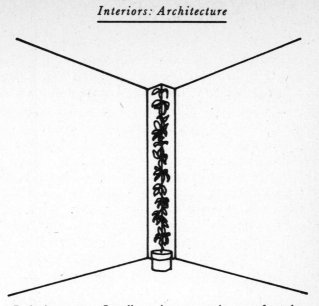

Projecting corner: Install a mirror or a vine to soften edge.

money in other ways. As a result, less and worse food will be set on the table. A rafter over a stove also affects wealth, curtailing financial opportunity.

Antidotes: Either move the bed, stove, or table out from under the beam, install an overheard mirror to allow ch'i to penetrate up through the beam, or place a firecracker above the beam to symbolically detonate the oppressive structure. Another, more mystical cure would be to hang two bamboo flutes slanting toward each other with red silk tassels or ribbons hanging down. Not only does this arrangement imitate the auspicious ba-gua formation—an image that corrects all wrongs—but because each flute is hollow, it becomes a purveyor of ch'i, symbolically rising through the beam. The flute is knifelike and if correctly aimed protects the occupants, chasing out evil spirits and tragedy.

In a hall, installing a false ceiling of translucent glass, lit by overhead lights, allows ch'i to circulate smoothly.

Avoid sharp, knifelike corners that jut into rooms, threatening occupants and undercutting their ch'i. The cure is to hang either a vine at the edge of the angle or a mirror on the side, or to round out the corner.

Even small objects jutting into close quarters can be detrimental. A U.S. government employee's office problems were traced to an attic handle hanging down in his hall. Although he worked hard and well, his boss always criticized him. The handle apparently programmed him to receive poor treatment: Every time he walked down the hall, he either had to duck or be grazed on the head, eventually molding his ch'i into a defensive, uneven shape and causing people to pick on him. Subconsciously the employee was asking for abuse. The antidote was, of course, to shorten the handle. Now, the employee reports office and home life are smoother. He works less, but his boss respects and treats him better. "I feel in control of my life."

STAIRS

Stairs are the house's conduits, pumping ch'i from one floor to the next. They should not be too confined. Graceful and rounded stairways curving into a main hall are best. (The Chinese avoid stairs running down straight toward the front door—this would allow good ch'i and financial opportunities to roll away.) Banisters with sharp angles can also hurt ch'i. Similarly, poorly lit low-lying ceilings over the stairs oppress ch'i, choking and inhibiting its flow upstairs. To enhance ch'i circulation, place a mirror on the ceiling, heightening the otherwise confining situation. Bright light can also activate stair and hall ch'i.

LIGHTS

Lights, symbolizing the sun, are auspicious. Dark rooms and halls oppress ch'i. Brightness stimulates a person's ch'i, bringing yang to a yin situation. The light should blend well with surroundings. For example, chandeliers both activate ch'i and distribute strong ch'i evenly around a room. If hung too low, or in the way of people's actions, however, they can harm the residents' ch'i.

MIRRORS

On Long Island, the Pans hang a mirror in the dining room not for design reasons but to improve feng shui. They want to draw the river water—money—into their home and onto their dining table, thus blessing their food and their lives. While mirrors, a frequent feng shui cure, are traditionally used to deflect evil spirits and bad feng shui formations, Black Hat feng shui uses mirrors in five additional ways: to draw in positive forces, such as water and mountain ch'i, and to refract light; to allow good ch'i to pass through unused doors, nourishing the apartment and the family; to reflect intruders when the occupant's back faces the door, preventing surprises that might disperse ch'i; to combat the oppressive effects of a close wall, thus creating a healthy visual sense of distance, so ch'i can circulate freely; and symbolically to bring inside the house a room that projects outside the front door.

Mirrors, no matter what the use, should never be hung so they cut off the top of the head of the tallest person in the family; otherwise, that person will be prone to headaches and his ch'i will be lowered. Similarly, mirrors should not be hung too high.

PLANTS

Plants provide an attractive panacea for many interior feng shui problems. They provide a symbolic reminder of both nature and growth, evoking nature in miniature. Placed in a corner, they allow ch'i to rise and circulate and not to linger. Placed at a protruding corner, they shield the room from sharp edges. Growing above the head of a bed, they elevate the sleeper's ch'i. Plants themselves, besides conducing ch'i, create and purvey it. They add a growing, lively feeling to a house. Often plants can curb malign affects, transforming it into smooth positive ch'i, such as restraining heavy ch'i doses that enter through large windows.

WATER

The presence of water in homes, offices, businesses, and restaurants draws in money. Some lucky companies with views of rivers, lakes, and harbors can hang mirrors to reflect water's money-giving ch'i into their businesses. Others, however, must supply their own water by installing fish tanks. (Ones with bubbles rising through them particularly stimulate ch'i circulation.) Water should always be clean and fish should be healthy.

Washrooms also are crucial to avoiding business going down the drain. At Lee Travel Service, the back door of the salesmen's office opened onto the entrance to the ladies' washroom. The office was advised to keep the door closed and to hang a half-length mirror to improve sales and to open up a symbolic new road.

In one Hong Kong business, the owner moved the washbasin—sink, pipes, and all—next to the accounts secretary. "Every time someone washes his hands," he explains, "more money comes in."

COLORS

Another aspect of good feng shui is color. To the Chinese, one's destiny can be shaded by the color of one's house, clothes, office, and so on. In the West, colors describe moods: seeing red, painting the town red, green with envy, feeling blue, white knight. Often one dresses in a color representing one's state of mind and feelings. Advertisers can often manipulate a person's emotional and psychological responses to a product by color choice. Similarly, color affects the feng shui of a home. Red, to the Chinese, is the most auspicious color, connoting happiness, fire or warmth, and strength. Shrines, clothes, and envelopes—the sort given to children on New Years or presented to geomancers for feng shui favors—are particularly special if they are red. A Chinese bride sports a scarlet cheongsam, the father of a newborn son hands out red eggs. Many of Lin Yun's patients wear red ribbons around wrists, waists, and necks to channel and retain ch'i.

Deep red and purple or plum—the "heart" of red—is an equally vital color, inspiring deep respect.

Green emits tranquility and freshness. It is the color of spring growth and a sign of healthy earth ch'i. Chu Mu, the movie director, lives in a green world surrounded by green upholstery, green rug, and plants. He even drives a green Mercedes. His reasons are more than just peace of mind. Explains Mr. Chu: "I was born in the year of the Ram and what do rams eat and thrive off of but grass, and the healthiest grass is green." So, living among green, Chu Mu hopes that his years will be fat and his opportunities will develop.

Yellow, the color of the sun and brightness, signifies longevity. A golden yellow was reserved for the imperial family in their clothes and ceramic tiles. Buddhist monks traditionally wear saffron-colored robes.

The most fearsome color to the Chinese is white. White is the deepest color of mourning: what black is to Western culture. At traditional Chinese funerals, the deceased's family shroud themselves in simple unbleached muslin robes as a sign of humble grief. Some say white dulls the senses. Stark, fashionable, white-on-white rooms signify death to the Chinese. When Lin Yun inspected an all-white artist's loft in the SoHo section of New York, he suggested that the door be painted red. Otherwise, he explained, "It's like a hospital or a sick-room—eventually family members will fall ill. You should have color." Many white interiors checked out by Lin Yun sport red flowers, red dots, red doors, green vines, or colorful rugs to offset a "white occurrence"—meaning death, failure, and sickness. In one Hong Kong dental clinic, attendants shunned the white uniform and agreed to work only after its color was switched to green.

One feng shui–fearing developer refuses to use white or blue—a cold, secondary mourning color—in his buildings, sticking to more auspicious greens and reds. (Blue is not always avoided.)

Black is also avoided. It signifies bad luck, dark happenings, the loss of light as the coffin door is finally closed.

Often color arrangement and outcome are quite specific. For a young man who wishes to marry, Lin Yun suggests a chu-shr cure: using pink sheets on the bed.

ROOM PLACEMENT

Room juxtaposition also affects feng shui. The closer the kitchen is to the dining room, for example, the better. The kitchen should also lie at a distance from the front door. The Chinese say if the guest enters and right away sees the kitchen, then the residence will constantly be used by friends dropping in only to eat. In such a case, keep the kitchen door closed with a mirror hung on it.

The siting of bathrooms is crucial. House plumbing seems to

affect the resident's internal plumbing and expenses, since the bathroom is the place where water—money—escapes from the house. Kitchens and bathrooms should be placed at a distance from each other. Otherwise, health and finance will be bad and earned money will seem spent or lost in no time. (Food money will be flushed away.) Keep the dining table closer to the kitchen.

If the first sight on entering a home is a bathroom, both guests and hosts will suffer from bad health. Also, the host's money will dwindle as finances get flushed away. Cure: Keep the door closed and hang a mrror on it.

A bathroom at the end of a long corridor is bad for a family's health, as it is right in the line of the arrowlike hall, conducting swift ch'i. Ch'i entering through a door or a window will shoot into the bathroom, affecting the family's biological systems. In one such household, the wife could not have children. A feng shui expert suggested, among other things, that she hang a beaded curtain in the corridor to disperse the ch'i. (A wind chime or mobile would also work.) A year later, she was a happy parent.

A toilet should never squarely face the door, but sit out of the main line of the door.

MAINTENANCE

House maintenance is crucial to the smooth flow of ch'i and the balance of yin and yang. A house in good shape best affects residents. Ch'i can alter as house fixtures—cracked windows, leaking roofs, cluttered halls and rooms, clogged plumbing—break down or wear out. The effect is similar to an aging or sickly body: If blood and breath cannot circulate, the rest of the body will be unhealthy. Upkeep is essential. Residents may suffer comparable ills. An unrepaired hole might fester, infecting residents who might then have to have an operation. Boxes and shopping bags piled up in a hall or behind a door may inhibit ch'i, thus blocking physical movement and career goals.

Door maintenance is important. A door must open easily. If the occupant must continually push to shove the stuck door open, the ch'i of his body becomes unbalanced. Doors must be well oiled. Shrill screeches of rusty hinges not only disperse interior ch'i, but also pierce the residents' ch'i, causing not only jumpy nerves but ill health. Doors must not bump into each other like gnashing teeth.

The condition of windows—the house's eyes, ears, and nostrils—can affect the occupant's health, particularly his orifices. If the window is broken or covered with paper, the occupant's ears, eyes, and nose will be uncomfortable. Childbearing will be difficult.

Bathroom upkeep is crucial. In Hawaii, a couple suffering from intestinal problems asked Lin Yun to look at their house. He noticed the bedroom did not have a door dividing it from the bathroom. The sink drain in the bathroom was clogged. He suggested that they unclog the sink and install a door, and once they had made these two repairs, the intestinal problems disappeared.

Seven

_____

INTERIORS: FURNITURE ARRANGEMENT

The Chinese resolve a multitude of interior problems, ranging from awkward room shapes to impractical kitchens, offices, and bedrooms, by rearranging furniture. Different arrangements give different impressions—furniture clustered together creates an intimate mood, a geometric array seems formal, other layouts seem homey. But the Chinese change their settings for other reasons, too, such as to harmonize unbalanced rooms and to alter both ch'i flow and, ultimately, the residents' destiny.

APARTMENT AND ROOM SHAPES

Apartment and room shapes follow rules of house and land shapes. Squares, rectangles, and circles are best. A shape can imply an innate destiny for residents. Death-oriented images are to be avoided. When a young couple moved into a new Hong Kong flat, they consulted a feng shui expert who advised them to move again because the living room walls were unparallel, connoting a coffin. The expert said unless they moved they would die. They ignored his advice, and shortly after, their Volkswagen plunged into a lake, killing both of them.

With unusually shaped apartments, the Chinese pay close attention to room placement. The bedroom, kitchen, and dining room should be within the main part of any house, and not in a wing projecting outside the front door. Avoid locating bedrooms and kitchens along the edge of a cleaver-shaped home or in the toe of a boot-shaped room.

Boot-shaped rooms and apartments can trip up occupants and suppress ch'i. In the summer of 1978, house-sitters had a feng shui expert over to the New York apartment of Gig Young and his wife. When he entered the apartment, he recalls, "I was overwhelmed by a sense of impending disaster. Several elements were awry." Not only was the apartment boot-shaped, but the bedrooms rested in the toe that projected outside the main door—a situation that en-

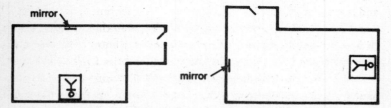

Knife-shaped or boot-shaped room: If the bed is against the edge or toe of these rooms, a mirror can draw the bed away from the dangerous wall.

courages disassociation in the family and the absence of the occupants. Moreoever, the bed itself rested right in the toe, resulting
in the stubbing of fate and career opportunities. The house-sitters
moved the bed out of the corner, but they left it in front of the door,
still in the wrong position. And, today, they blame the Youngs'
curious deaths on the mysterious workings of bad feng shui.

With a cleaver-shaped house or room, a bed, stove, or desk
should not be placed on the cutting edge. However, if furniture is
strategically arranged in the handle—the controlling part of the
knife—the occupants will be in greater charge of their own lives. For
example, proper manipulation of a cleaver-shaped room can give

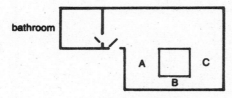

Mah-jongg room.

those who never seem to win at games, be it poker or Parcheesi, an
edge over opponents: The cleaver shape of a mah-jongg room in the
house of actor Patrick Tse and his actress wife Debbie Lee means
good luck for some players and bad luck for others, depending on
where they sit. Miss Lee explains: "One friend always wins. Usually, he sits in seat B. Last time he won $800. Then he sat in seat A
and lost half of it. In seat C, he lost more." Apparently, seat A is the
worst because it rests on the cutting blade, inhibiting its occupant's
ch'i so he/she plays poorly. One antidote is to move the table out
from the blade wall. A chu-shr guarantee for Miss Lee to win is for
her to go into the bathroom (the handle of the knife) and wash her
hands, thus ritually acquiring control of the money situation.
Another strategy is to let the table, bed, desk, or stove rest against
the blade, and to hang a mirror on the opposite wall to reflect the
furniture away from the edge.

The Chinese also avoid strange-angled rooms. A room with an angle smaller than ninety degrees is unbalanced with an uneven ch'i flow. Such an angle will trap ch'i, causing business to fail and creating a dead end for luck. To remedy this, install a tree or flowering plant in the corner to allow ch'i to go through the plant, because plants give life to otherwise dead ch'i and recirculate it.

FURNITURE PLACEMENT

Bedrooms

Because most people spend at least a third of their lives in bed, the bed position can shape ch'i. The first consideration is the bed's juxtaposition to the door. Always place a bed cater-corner to the bedroom door so that one lying in the bed can see who is entering. (The Chinese avoid having a bed's feet aim at the door, which resembles coffins in mortuaries, thus evoking forebodings of death.) If the cater-corner arrangement is impossible, hang a mirror to reflect any intruder who might startle the occupant and disperse his/her ch'i. Avoid overhead beams and knifelike corners that overhang or point toward the bed. A headboard should be higher than the footboard.

Large bureaus and armoires, if placed next to or near the foot of the bed, can also imbalance the occupant's ch'i, inhibiting body

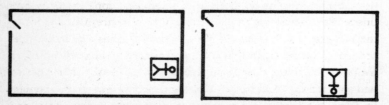

Ideal bedroom: Bed should be cater-corner to the door.

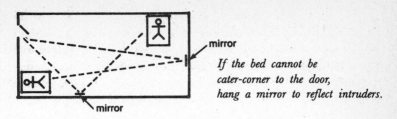

mirror

If the bed cannot be cater-corner to the door, hang a mirror to reflect intruders.

mirror

movements and disturbing internal harmony. The effect on children can be more severe. For example, in the crowded quarters where three sisters slept—a double-decker bunk and a cramped cot—a feng shui man asked the girls, "Who broke her arm in the past few months?" It was the girl in the cramped bed.

. In the room of a Western journalist's son, a heavy bureau flanked the bed. The feng shui expert asked about a recent broken arm. And the couple said yes, he just broke his arm, and the next week, their son broke his arm again.

The Chinese feel the shape of a bed can mold a marriage. A bed with rounded corners can take the edges out of a rocky marriage. A communal large mattress is better than two twin-sizes lying side-by-side. One American journalist took heart when a feng shui man said the rifts with his wife could be patched up by replacing their twin beds with a king-size mattress. By getting rid of the crack between their beds, the expert said, the chasm of their conflicts would be bridged.

Beds should generally rest against a wall. Otherwise, the occupant will feel unstable with nothing to lean on in life.

During pregnancy, to avoid miscarriages, don't move or dust under beds. According to the chu-shr view of conception and birth, the universe is full of *ling,* or spirits. Each ling has a character and seeks out chances to enter the woman's womb to give life-breath to the fetus. When the child is born, the spirit will be the child's breath and aura (ch'i). These ling float under beds, waiting for the moment to enter the womb. If the woman is always arranging things and cleaning, ling will scatter and the fetus will be lost.

Bed placement can be the outcome of minute calculations. It can be determined by detailed astrology and numerology. The bed can be positioned according to the ba-gua: A bed facing north means business will be good; facing northeast brings on intelligence and learning; east means family life will be happy, rewarding, and peaceful; southeast indicates wealth; south will bring in fame; southwest means a good spouse and happy marital relations; west promises fame for future generations; northwest indicates travel far and wide. Charles Dickens always slept facing east, in order to catch the most positive cosmic flow.

Other mystified Westerners have come around to using feng shui in bedrooms. One British woman married to a Chinese says: "We moved into a house in Bangkok—which has its own brand of feng shui—and everything went wrong. You couldn't put your finger on it but we said, 'Here we are, a happy couple, yet nothing is happy around us'—arguments, relationships, all were going wrong. So a feng shui man told us: 'Ah, your bed is in the wrong position.' But we didn't change it." Five months went on and things got worse. "Then one day my husband marched into the bedroom and moved the bed into the corner of the room. It was an extraordinary experience—perhaps it was merely in my mind—but, suddenly, everything went right."

Sometimes rooms can be cursed with multiple problems. Dr. Liang, for example, practicing Western medicine in Hong Kong, could not sleep. "I'm not comfortable in bed," he said. "Does the bed have a problem? Should I change the mattress? Is it too soft?" None of the above. A beam running lengthwise over the Liangs' bed made them feel something was going on over their heads, making them anxious. A feng shui man suggested hanging two flutes in a ba-gua arrangement on the beam. In addition, outside the building runs a road that aims at the building and then curves around it, appearing to enter through one window, run over the bed, and go out another window. Dr. Liang asked, "Should I keep the windows closed?" To disperse the unsettling road ch'i, the feng shui expert suggested wind chimes be hung at the center crosspoint of the room.

Living Rooms

Living rooms are less complicated, as they are receiving rooms for guests. However, they should be light and large and devoid of feng shui ills such as beams, oddly shaped corners and angles, or three windows or doors in a row. The host's favorite chair should face the entrance.

Living rooms should contain certain shapes, pictures, and doodads imbued with symbolic powers with which the resident identifies, such as ba-gua–shaped rugs or rounded tables. Chu Mu went "whole-hog" in this department. Not only are the corners and bed edges rounded, but also his desk, dining table, stairway, and couch—even a moon door that he claims can stop disaster. "Rounded decor to Westerners may be interior design, but to Chinese it is also feng shui," explains Mr. Chu. "If prosperity comes, it could go out the front door. This way wealth circulates through the house."

Chinese homes, restaurants, and stores also hang watercolors of flowers and plants, such as peonies, which symbolize peace and long life.

In the doodad department, Chu Mu's living room is infested with good luck paraphernalia. There rests a pantheon of fat smiling Buddhas to improve the ch'i throughout the flat and to attract wealth; an Eiffel Tower and a seashell schooner to ensure travel to far places and wide-reaching distribution of his movies; a knife fashioned of old Chinese coins, strung together with red string, to protect Mr. Chu from misfortune; and a trio of ivory Taoist sages to attract luck, fame, and money.

KITCHEN: HOME AND RESTAURANT

The Chinese pay attention to the kitchen, especially the placement of the stove and rice cooker. Stoves are the symbolic sources of fortune because food is cooked there. (The Chinese word for food, *tsai*, sounds the same as their word for wealth.) In addition, food affects health, emotions, and behavior, so gastronomic satisfaction is crucial. Says Lin Yun, "From our food comes health and effectiveness. If it is well prepared and of good quality, we will do well in the world, earn more money to buy even better food." This food-money cycle, however, can turn the other way. "If you are poor, you eat worse, then fare poorly in the world. You might perform so poorly that eventually you get fired." The Chinese aren't the only ones to feel this way. As Virginia Woolf wrote after a less-than-agreeable meal: "One cannot think well, love well or sleep well, if one has not dined well. The lamp in the spine does not light on beef and prunes."*

The stove should not be in a cramped corner, inhibiting the cook's ch'i, but should allow the cook room to work. Otherwise, the chef might constantly hit her elbow, unbalancing her ch'i. In this case, mirrors can visually extend the space.

Above the stove, many Chinese hang a picture of the kitchen god who watches over the family and the hearth. A sort of spy for heaven, every New Year's he makes a journey up to the skies to report on the family. Before he embarks, he is bribed with food offerings and his mouth is smeared with honey so he will say only sweet things about the family.

Other kitchen hazards are angles pointing dangerously at the cook. In this case, hang either a mirror or something growing, such as a vine, to soften the edge.

---

*Virginia Woolf, *A Room of One's Own* (New York: Harcourt, Brace & World, 1957), p. 18.

The best stove site is where the toiling cook can see all entering the kitchen. Interaction is thus smooth. If a cook faces away from the door, health, wealth, and domestic harmony will suffer. Surprises disperse the cook's ch'i, making him or her jumpy, and the meal disappointing, thus affecting the whole household. "It makes sense," comments a Chinese-American State Department employee. "The husband comes home and surprises the wife in the kitchen; she might snap at him and a senseless fight will ensue." One precaution is to hang a mirror above the stove so the cook can see—Annie Oakley-style—any intruder, or to hang a bell or wind chime near the door so that before the visitor enters, he knocks against it.

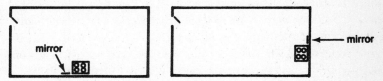

Stove sites: In the kitchen, avoid having the cook's back to the door. Hang a mirror to reflect intruders.

This is particularly important in restaurants. If the chef is surprised, a nervous chain reaction is set off, affecting everything from his performance to the waiters' attitudes to the customers' satisfaction. If ch'i circulation is smooth, it improves the quality of the dishes and the amount of business. (In one New York restaurant, however, the chef declined to have a feng shui mirror installed above his stove because, he said, it made him dizzy.)

Throughout Asia and the United States, Chinese restaurants use feng shui. Some of New York City's choicest Chinese restaurants—David K's, Hunam, Peng's, to mention a few—have been scrutinized and sanctified by a feng shui expert. The approach is both culinary and business-oriented. In 1978, the part-owner of Peking Park, Lawrence Chow, sent Lin Yun a round-trip Hong Kong–New York ticket to check out his restaurant's feng shui. Not only had business been poor, but a review by Mimi Sheraton, the *New York Times* restaurant critic, bestowed only a one-star rating. "I can't understand it. We have first-class chefs," remarked Mr. Chow. Hoping to stem his restaurant's losing streak, Mr. Chow invited a feng shui man, who divined that the restaurant's problem lay in the position of the cash register. They moved it closer to the door to improve the flow of money. Less than a year later, Gael Greene gave the restaurant a two-star rating in *New York* magazine.

Ch'i flow affects a restaurant's business. A feng shui rule is to create a good atmosphere for clients: angles, for example, abuse customers and create financial obstacles for owners. In Washington's House of Hunan, owner Johnny Kao covered a row of square columns with mirrors to allow ch'i to circulate evenly and to diminish the sharp effect of the columns' angles. He also installed round bar-counter ends.

In general, the cash register should be cater-corner to the entrance so the cashier faces the customers. A mirror should be installed to ensure the influx of business and money.

Restaurants can benefit from symbolic decor. Many Chinese restaurants choose the auspicious mixture of red and gold, symbolizing good luck and fortune. Their walls are festooned with pictures of Taoist sages and gods, flowers and landscapes—images that connote longevity, peace, and prosperity. Often these are enhanced by "double happiness," "long life," and "prosperity" written in gold characters on a red background. Other symbolism can be more subtle: fish tanks, meaning money, or plants, meaning growing ch'i. At a popular New York sushi bar, Lin Yun noted that the appealing decor of hollow vertical bamboo stalks helped the restaurant thrive. "Like large flutes they channel up and activate ch'i." In New York, David Keh, owner of David K's, added several large fish tanks to improve ch'i and to drum up even more business.

STORES

Shopkeepers in Asia and the United States also use feng shui. Some stores sport small altars with pictures of the god of wealth. The Hong Kong and Shanghai Bank painted a god of wealth high above its old trading floor. In Sunnyside, Queens, Julie Wu invited a feng shui man to look at her newly bought cleaning store. She explains, "For twenty-eight years, the former owners weren't prosperous." The problems came from a slanted door and the position of the cash register. After hanging a mirror behind the register, putting a wind chime near the door, and placing plants by the slanted door and corners, business improved.

Stores also follow domestic feng shui rules. A jewelry store proprietress in Hong Kong hangs a plastic vine on a dangerously sharp corner in her shop to both smooth the corner's edge and siphon up ch'i.

Plastic, silk, and paintings of plants also improve surroundings and business. While walking through Saks Fifth Avenue, in New York, Lin Yun commented that a display of fake trees that appeared to grow out of sales counters increased the department store's business. "Trees give the feeling of springtime, when all is blooming," he said. "So the store will develop and prosper." He added that they elevated and helped ch'i circulate, making people flock to shop there.

STUDIES AND OFFICES

In studies, desks should sit cater-corner to the door with the occupant facing the door. If one prefers looking out on an inspiring view, which precludes facing the door, a mirror may be hung above the desk angled to reflect any intruder. In Hong Kong, a reporter thought his work would improve if he hung a mirror above his desk

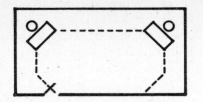

Two desks in a study create a ba-gua symbol.

that looked out on the South China Sea—in addition to attaining the ch'i of the water outside, his own ch'i would not be hurt from being startled, so he could retain his train of thought.

If two people have to work in one room, as academics C. C. Lee and his wife do, the desks can be placed to create a ba-gua shape with the wall. A plant and a bright lamp in back·of the desks may create an aura to improve ch'i.

Next to the home, office arrangement is the most essential in determining a person's fortunes. Throughout Asia, many businesses, both Chinese and expatriate, call on feng shui experts to inspect their premises. Among them: Chase Asia, American Chamber of Commerce (Amcham), Citibank, the *Asian Wall Street Journal,* Jardines, and so forth. Some multinationals are known to auspiciously position each employee's desk according to astrology to encourage higher productivity and greater prosperity. When the *Far Eastern Economics Review* moved into a new office, they enlisted the help of a feng shui man. He said three desks were inauspiciously placed. Derek Davies, the *Review*'s managing editor, writes:

> One belonging to the receptionist Helen Tung, who had been feeling off-color since the move, was switched around and adorned with a "good luck" character—and she immediately perked up. "Focus" editor Donald Wise, who has otherwise hardly known a day's illness but who had been struck down with pleurisy and gout (twice!) since the move, trundled his desk across the editorial floor—and also recovered.

Other desks facing east, south or northeast were duly adorned with red porcelain horses or dark marble flower pots, filled with water but no flowers. I rotated my south-facing desk 15 degrees clockwise.*

The first consideration in any office is the manager's desk. Applying the theory that a country's destiny is determined by the feng shui of the emperor's palace, especially his throne, the Chinese feel the entire company's fortunes rest on the good siting of its president or manager. Some Hong Kong residents say Jardines encountered problems when a new director took over but failed to have his office adjusted by a feng shui expert.

The manager should reside in the most commanding position to assert his authority over his employees. Authority generally emits from the corner office farthest from the entrance. American office

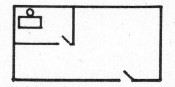

Ideal office and seat for manager.

arrangement also coincides with feng shui. In *Power!*, Michael Korda writes: "Generally speaking, offices are based upon a corner power system, rather than a central one. . . . the closer one is to the center the less powerful one is."† However, in feng shui not any corner will do. The manager of the Lee Travel Service in Kowloon, Frank Kwok, moved his office from the north to the south side—an old conference room—so that he would sit in a position fitting his rank. His second-in-command moved into his old office, and a wall

Far Eastern Economics Review (February 2, 1979), p. 27.
†Michael Korda, *Power!* (New York: Random House, 1975), p. 75.

was knocked down enabling her to oversee workers in an adjacent room.

Offices often follow apartment rules: avoiding knifelike corners, beams, columns, long dark hallways. Offices sited at the end of a long corridor—peering into the dragon's mouth—are undesirable. In such a case, move desks away from the dragon's mouth or install a screen to fend off the strong ch'i. Sometimes, screens can cover up for inside corruption. A Taiwan construction manager added a mirror to the screen, symbolically discouraging workers froom double-dealing behind his back.

Desks should sit cater-corner to doors. As Michael Korda explains, "Even among the highest and most securely protected of the executive elite, it is usual for the desk to be positioned so that its occupant can look up and see the door, not so much out of politeness as because nobody likes to be caught unawares."[*]

In feng shui terms, being startled from one's work unbalances ch'i, making one jumpy, easy to upset, and partially distracted, thus impairing one's work. Robert Upton, assistant regional director of the New Territories, comments, "When I first moved into my office, I sat with my back to the door." Now he sits where he can see everyone entering. "They tell me it gives me 'killing ch'i,' so I am better equipped to handle matters, and in fact, things *are* much better." (This position is further defended by a ba-gua mirror on his window, deflecting malign forces from the adjacent police station.) There are, however, exceptions: His boss, David Akers-Jones, is quite content to officiate from a seat chosen by a feng shui expert—with his back to the door.

Most offices should have doors on them. A windowed door is a disadvantage: Everyone entering can see the occupant first, thus putting him or her on the defensive. If a desk cannot be cater-corner to the door, hang a mirror to reflect anyone entering. (Some carry

[*]*Ibid.,* p. 79.

their symbolic search for superiority too far, with high seats for them and low chairs for visitors. Deals and bargaining edges have been lost by a visitor making the mistake of sinking into a fluffy sofa.)

In Hong Kong, stories proliferate about feng shui men picking out a "hexed" seat where an occupant died or failed. One such case happened in the architecture office of Eric Cumine. "I had a feng shui man in before office hours. He said there was one very bad seat—a jinxed seat." Mr. Cumine found this quite remarkable because the seat's last occupant, his son, had died only two months before. (The next occupant of the jinxed seat didn't believe in feng shui, even after his aunt and sister died suddenly.) The geomancer pointed to two seats, saying they were never "warm." And, indeed, those were the seats of trainees who would stay with the firm for a year, then quit to join the government planning office or another firm. Mr. Cumine noted he and his partner sit in the best seats—the way it should be.

Often, however, feng shui is a convenient excuse for doing poorly in business. The son of a Chinese film producer commented that his father always blames his box-office failures on bad feng shui and credits his smash business successes to his own talent. A man working for Chase Asia blamed feng shui for his poor performance at the bank. When the bank refused to relocate his desk, he left in protest—some say he was going to be fired anyway.

Some businessmen follow their feng shui expert's every word, occasionally to their own loss. One expatriate businessman married to a Chinese woman fared very well financially and was therefore in awe of his geomancer. One day the geomancer overheard the wife asking, "Why do you always follow that feng shui man's advice? You're European—I'm Chinese and I don't believe in that rubbish." So when the husband consulted with the geomancer, the geomancer said, "You are a very lucky man. You have lots of money and a good business. However, you could be twice as rich as you are. One thing stands in your way—your wife. To fulfill your great destiny you must send her away for six months every year."

So the wife, against her wishes, was shuttled off on safaris, tours, and shopping sprees for half a year. And for a while the husband thrived. But, eventually, his luck—not to mention his marriage—failed.

At times, office feng shui maneuvering can create tense office politics. When Unicom, United Press International's commodity wire service, set up office in Hong Kong, its American manager called in a feng shui man. He said that in the office Unicom shared with trouble-ridden UPI—one editor had broken an arm, others suffered marital problems, people left, others got sick—the bad ch'i emanated from the acting bureau chief's office. To deflect this, the manager hung a large mirror that caused further office problems: UPI's Chinese teletypists claimed the evil spirits were reflected in their direction and hung three octagonal mirrors fortified with hexing forks facing Unicom. Applying rank, the manager insisted the teletypists' mirror be removed.

Eight

HOUSE SPIRITS

Moving into a house or an office is like stepping into the previous owner's shoes. A desirable house is one in which the former tenant prospered and was content. Even better is one in which the family's fortunes were so good that they moved into larger and grander quarters. In such lucky cases, feng shui men claim, the next residents might well follow in their footsteps, aligning their fortunes with their predecessors'. Often new residents will repeat what happened to former tenants within two or three years.

This hand-me-down destiny has its obvious pitfalls: A former tenant may have died, gotten divorced, lost money, or argued with his family. And the resonances of these experiences may linger and affect the new occupant.

When moving into a house or an office, the Chinese investigate its past—who lived there and what happened. One puzzled New York real estate agent commented that some Chinese clients took great interest in houses' histories and—to be safe—avoided old ones, where the chance of a death in former households was greater. (Indeed, like a cookie cutter, bad interior feng shui—an ill-placed bathroom, an arrowlike corner, or a drafty hall—will re-create problems.)

In these cases, a feng shui man or a Buddhist priest is often consulted. These experts are purportedly endowed with a sense about previous owners and events. Beyond offering practical advice—furniture arrangement, door and window alignment, orientation—which may well have a scientific base, they explore an additional intangible aspect, the house spirit. This dimension is harder to define and prove than the effect of an oppressive beam; it addresses such nonverifiable realities as the sensations people get from a house.

CONSECRATING A HOUSE

Any dwelling or building, whether it is old or new, well-placed or not, needs a moving-in ceremony, a consecration. A feng shui priest is called in to perform, with the aid of incense and chants, the first rites of the company, home, or shop. The consecration serves as both a cure for problems ranging from poor finances to bad architecture and a ritual warding off of potential ills and evil spirits. Often the ceremonies serve to attract clients, letting locals know a company is open for business. The Hong Kong and Shanghai Bank stages Dragon Dances when opening a new branch, even at the

World Trade Center in New York. As one bank official comments, "Who are we to fly in the face of superstition?"

House consecration dates back to the Shang dynasty, when dogs, humans, cows, and so forth were sacrificed and placed under a shrine or stele to spiritually guard a home, village, or palace.

One modern example is the Chase Asia building. For years, wags in Hong Kong joked that Chase Asia, Chase Manhattan Bank's merchant banking arm, was far less successful in its financial transactions than its rival, Citibank, due to feng shui. The Citibank building is well positioned at the confluence of two roads. At first, people blamed Chase's problems on the old Chase Asia building, not only because it was nestled in formerly malaria-infested land and had a graveyard as a next-door neighbor but also for the building's six-sided windows which bore a close resemblance to coffins. In 1978 the company moved to a new building. (It is unclear exactly why they moved, though some locals suspect a feng shui motive.)

But Chase's problems increased. The building had never been consecrated by an appropriate priest. After Chase Asia lost four big deals in a row and then lost a senior executive in a plane crash, it enlisted a feng shui expert. The two trouble spots, he said, were in the executive director's office and a manager's office. The director was quoted as saying of the solution, "I don't mind. It means I get fresh red flowers every day on my desk to chase away the devils." The other manager? "He got goldfish. They keep dying, but they're supposed to—to keep the devils busy." The fact that the company has since been prospering is "purely coincidental."

Even Dow Chemical does not hedge its bets, as UPI reported:

At Dow Chemical, a feng shui expert held the opening ceremony of a plant during a week of pouring rain. A threatened deluge held off until after the outdoor extravaganza for 300 guests. The executive who organized the event, Dean Wakefield, the marketing communications director, was congratulated by Chinese executives—not for avoiding soaked dignitaries but for the downpour that followed. The rain signified that "the money can't wait to pour down on you." Mr. Wakefield said that the venture has been successful beyond the company's expectations.*

One Black Hat feng shui method of mystical housewarming to establish ownership and right to the apartment space is to place nine orange, lemon, or lime skins in a bowl or pail. Fill it with water. Then splash the citrus water on all floors—where there is wall-to-wall carpeting use an atomizer—cleansing the place of bad ch'i and evil spirits. (A Western-educated Chinese said whenever he moves into a new apartment, he turns on the radio full blast as if saying, "There, spirits, I'm here now and you can kindly leave.") On the first day of moving in, take a flute, symbolizing a sword, and a flower vase, symbolizing security and peace, with a red ribbon wrapped around its neck. Enter the house carrying the vase and the flute. Walk through each room to establish one's presence.

Firecrackers should be used all over the house, especially in the front entrance. (When a member of a household dies, his offspring sets off firecrackers at the entrance to shoo away the deceased's ghost.)

After moving into a new house, avoid sleeping on an old bed. If this is impossible, however, buy new sheets and bedspread to give a fresh feeling for a good start.

As times change, so can the feng shui of a house. This depends on how the patterns of ch'i fluctuate. Sometimes a house's ch'i may become more auspicious or it may sour. As in the Chinese concept of the universe, a home's ch'i will also vary. Although one hundred years ago a house might possess good ch'i, the constant fluctuation of the universal tides, outside events, and development and depletion of environmental resources can inhibit the strength and flow of ch'i and a family's luck may go downhill.

*Suzanne Green, United Press International, September 1977.

Lucy Lo, a cooking instructor and Hong Kong philanthropist, explains, "About ten years ago, there were so many deaths in my family. After the first one, I didn't take notice. Then my mother died, then my brother. I started to get nervous, then came the fourth death." So she consulted the family feng shui scholar, who said, "Your house already has fifty years of good luck, from now on the luck is finished," and advised her to move.

At first Ms. Lo didn't believe him and didn't move. "But, then, my father-in-law died, so all the old folk had died. The young people decided to move. So I moved, too."

The fear of ghosts is a factor connected to a house's feng shui. The Chinese believe in a parallel world in which spirits exist at the side of the living. Chinese ghosts have power over the living, so various festivals, such as grave-sweeping, or the festival of the hungry ghosts, are devoted to keeping them content and out of trouble. Places where the Japanese are known to have imprisoned, tortured, or killed people have acquired the stigma of bad feng shui. Although the spirit-placating Tun Fu ceremony is mostly limited to rural areas, this odd exorcism still occurs in more developed sectors. In Indonesia, when one American-owned company suffered financial setbacks, local company officials insisted the factory was haunted. However, after the Americans agreed to sacrifice a sheep and roasted it on the plant's steps, it appeared that the problem was less ghosts than money being spirited off by employees.

Some Chinese believe the Hong Kong government is not immune to "hauntings." In 1974, the Murray Road Carpark was the scene of an exorcism rite financed by the colony's transport department. The bureau's headquarters were to be housed above the parking lot. The building, workers said, rests on a site where Japanese tortured people in World War II. So thirty years later a parade of seventy Buddhist priests, chanting and burning incense, pacified their spirits. As reported in the *South China Morning Post*, the Reverend Koh Kwang, president of the Buddhist Association, claimed, "The service will not only be able to pacify spirits, but also be able to extend its blessings to the smooth operation of transport without any major accidents."

The fear of haunted places often affects house prices and rents. In a lovely area of Singapore known to be a site of World War II tortures, a large house will rent for U.S. $750 per month. Only Westerners dare to live there. Prime real estate and beautiful old houses in crowded Hong Kong, where space is a precious commodity, lie fallow because of either ghosts or mere bad feng shui. Prospective buyers are often tempted by low prices, but usually think twice if the house possesses bad feng shui or ghosts.

On Hong Kong Island, one old mansion sited on expensive land remained abandoned for years. The story: Soon after an amah drowned in a bathtub, residents heard strange noises, a chair started rocking on its own, and objects were mysteriously moved around at night. The family moved. The house was eventually bought by the PRC, but, locals claim, even they called in an exorcist. Despite this gesture, however, amahs will work only during daylight hours.

Nine

CONCLUSION

Feng shui covers a vast area of human endeavor. Along with direct-ing the destinies of countries, families, and individuals, it also deals with the minutiae of everyday life. At this level, feng shui can be highly personalized, depending on individual needs, desires, and criteria. It may deal with names, astrology, numbers and a concept called the five elements (see Appendix 5). When home and office rearrangements are insufficient solutions, the chu-shr mystical cures are often called for: In New York, a young writer placed his manuscript on a high armoire to ensure a book contract; the owner of a popular New York Chinese restaurant jiggled his full cash register to shake up even more business. A bank employee rubbed a mixture of wine and a Chinese herbal powder on her sole to heal an ailing liver. Even former Vice-President Spiro Agnew has been seen in the company of a feng shui man, presumably seeking advice. Chu-shr cures number in the thousands. Their potency comes from being transmitted orally only after a red "lucky money" packet is presented to the feng shui man. To maintain the cure's mystical powers, the "client" must not reveal details of the cure until success is achieved. Any "leaks" or secret-sharing diminish the power.

Feng shui is still a mystery. Sometimes it may parallel modern ideas of physics, self-fulfilling prophecy, medicine, and even just plain good design. At other times, however, logical explanations fall short. With a bit of his own brand of irrationality, Lin Yun asserts that in feng shui, ru-shr at best achieves 10 percent success, while the results of transcendental chu-shr can be as high as 120 percent. For example, if a couple is embroiled in a marital crisis, the normal advice is to show respect, be patient, and be more loving and considerate of each other. This is ru-shr—reasonable, logical, and easy to accept. But, as much as people would like to be considerate and work things out, the results are only 10 percent effective. In using chu-shr, a couple might reverse or adjust their bed a bit. Although it seems illogical and irrational, an act of mere faith, the impact will be far greater than the results from ru-shr.

With an approach that is both sensitive and knowledgeable, Black Hat feng shui encompasses both ru-shr—this-worldly, rational, and logical—and chu-shr—transcendent, irrational, and illogical. Similar to ru-shr, feng shui includes everything within our scope of experience and knowledge: scientific discoveries, facts, and understood events. And similar to chu-shr, feng shui is also the great expanse outside our known world: What is yet to happen, to be discovered, understood, or seen.

Appendix 1

THE TUN FU CEREMONY

Details of Tun Fu ceremony performed at Pak Wai village, January 17, 1960, as reported by G. C. W. Grout, a government officer in the New Territories. The geomancer's name was Cheung Yuen Chong and he comes from Kwangsi Province.

"He started by placing the incense, the cups and the rice bowl and red packet on a table. . . . The incense was then lit and water placed in the rice bowl. Two pieces of joss paper were then lit, placed in the rice bowl of water, and the nail put into it. He then took up one of the pieces of wet bamboo, passed it over the burning incense and wrote certain secret inscriptions on it, copying out of the book, and passed it over the incense again, the written side down.

"This was repeated for each piece of bamboo. Then the red cloth was cut into strips and tied with red string, and gilt leaves to the top of the inscribed bamboos. The inscriptions seemed to be in pairs, three pieces with different writing on the right and again three on the left, similarly written.

"After this was done, wine was poured into three cups and tea poured in the other three, the candles lit, and the geomancer took up his position at the head of the table and started his incantations.

"After about five minutes of prayer he seized the young live cockerel by the head in his left hand, and taking hold of the nail from the rice bowl, plunged it into the cockerel's eye. On the impact the young cockerel almost struggled free, fighting so hard that the geomancer had to tighten his grip and to push the nail in its eye once more. With a crunching noise he pierced the nail right through the cockerel's head and out of the other eye. Thereupon, the cockerel ceased struggling and lay limp, as if dead.

"Still holding the cockerel with the nail through its head in his left hand, he ordered the V.R. [village representative] and his assistant to place the bamboos in the two pots with sand, three in each pot with a cup of tea. He sprinkled some of the blood from the cockerel's eyes on the bamboos and then nailed the cockerel on to a tree, suspended by this nail through its eyes. Joss paper was then burnt under the tree, wine was poured on the ground in front of the tree, and crackers were fired.

"The geomancer then took the cockerel off the tree and more crackers were fired. Holding it in his left hand, he pulled the nail out with his right, and put some water from the rice bowl in the cockerel's blinded eyes with his finger. Crackers were set off again. The limp cockerel was placed on the ground and the geomancer then filled his mouth with water from the rice bowl and blew on the cockerel twice, hitting it on the rump at the same time. Surprisingly enough, the cockerel got up and started staggering about, not knowing where to go, as it was still dazed and couldn't see.

"One of the pots with the three bamboos was then taken up by the V.R. on the geomancer's instructions. They brought it to the end of the village and placed it under a tree chosen by the geomancer. The assistant then went with a pick and started digging into the hillside behind the village at intervals of about 10 feet. Then the other pot with the other three bamboos was taken to the other end of the village and similarly placed.

"Lastly, the geomancer declared that work could start in three days' time and said the ceremonies were over.

"P.S. The V.R. came into our office two days later and I asked him about the cockerel. He said it was quite healthy and could see. I said I didn't believe him and asked to see the victim that afternoon. He had a good laugh and explained that the nail was stuck in the eye socket in such a way as to avoid the eye. I still insisted and arranged to see it that afternoon. It looked quite healthy and appeared to be the same one. On closer examination I found that one eye was blinded. Apparently the geomancer fumbled a bit."

Appendix 2

NAMES

As Shakespeare once asked, "What's in a name?" A great deal, according to many Chinese. They attach great significance to the literal and implied images of place names. They named hills and mountains, of course, after their shapes. But names can change as man transforms his landscape. A place in Hong Kong used to be called "Green Dragon Head" because the landscape resembled a dragon. About one hundred years ago, the story goes, a farmer discovered a pair of round, glasslike rocks buried under the earth. He dug them out and yellow water gushed out profusely. Locals say the farmer had offended feng shui. Soon after, he fell ill and died. From then on, locals referred to the area by an updated name, "Blind Dragon."

Chinese is a homonymous language; names and words constantly evoke portents and symbols that the Chinese fear will eventually become reality. For example, a newlywed couple living in a New Territories area with a name originally translated as meaning "twin trees"—which through years of British mispronunciation of Cantonese sounded more like "separated lovers" or, even worse, "twin corpses"—were advised by a feng shui expert to move, for fear of their lives and marriage.

Historically, place names have caused problems for Westerners. When the British wanted to introduce telegraph lines linking Hong Kong and Kowloon to Canton, the people at the Cantonese end were not amused by this development. They said the telegraph wires would mark the decline of Canton and bring possible disaster. Canton, alias the City of Rams, would be tethered and led by the leashlike telegraph lines right to the mouths of nine hungry dragons (Kowloon).

Even the Hong Kong Tourist Association credits the Chinese name of Bruce Lee, the late king of kung fu movies, with his untimely death in 1973. At the time of his death, Lee, whose Chinese name was Lee Shao-lung, "Little Dragon," lived in a Hong Kong suburb called Kowloon Tong, "Pond of the Nine Dragons." A Tourist Association press release notes, "Had he consulted a feng shui master before moving in, it is likely that he would have been warned against tempting fate. For in the mythological survival of the fittest, the little dragon must eventually give way to the combined might of the nine full-grown creatures who dominate the legendary pond."

Reports say Lee knew of the bad feng shui and sought to deflect it by hanging the octagonal ba-gua mirror outside his front door. But people say that the mirror was blown off during a typhoon shortly before the actor's death, leaving him undefended against the inevitable.

The Chinese devoted great thought to selecting the name for a capital. The Chinese empire's first capital, Chang-an, "long peace," lasted nearly a millennium.

Appendix 3

NUMBERS

To the Chinese, as to other cultures, numbers possess magical powers. Renaissance poets such as Edmund Spenser arranged lyrics and syllables in numerological schemes to bring a subconscious sense of harmony to the reader. In the West we have three wishes in fairy tales, the Christian Trinity, and the sacred restorative powers of pyramids (four triangles). Seven and nine also recur as numbers in magical ceremonies throughout the world.

As in the West, the Chinese traditionally used what they considered auspicious numbers in their architecture. For example, in a chapter on "Building Artisanship" in the *Rites of Chou,* a book on Chou dynasty ritual practices, the repetition of particularly auspicious numbers further sanctified a capital city. "The capital shall measure nine *li* (a Chinese mile) on each side and on each side there shall be three gates. Within the city, there shall be nine north-south streets and nine east-west streets. The north-south streets shall accommodate nine chariot ways."*

Other architectural examples range from the imperial palace in Peking, which is based on "magic squares," and the Temple of Heaven (*Ming Tang*, literally translated as "cosmic house"), which has steps built in variables of three and nine.

The Chinese took great care to measure and build their temples according to the strict numerological calculations of geomancers. Miscalculations, they believed, would jeopardize not only the temple's sacred powers but also the worshiper's fortunes—some temples were abandoned because of slight slips of the ruler.

"Nine" and "one" are the most auspicious Chinese numbers. Nine connotes fullness, it is the largest number. One signifies the beginning, the birth.

The Chinese in Hong Kong and Taiwan interpret even more meanings into numbers than traditional magic. The sounds of numbers, as of names, are associated with other meanings. Homonyms add a special significance to Chinese numbers. A parallel to this would be if Americans started to identify *won* with the symbol *one*.

This practice extends to many areas of life in Asia. A Hong Kong artist picked a date to open her painting exhibit because the numbers added up to nine, which in Mandarin means "long life." A real estate developer could not sell certain office lots in a multimillion-dollar development because they ended in four, which in Cantonese sounds like "die." Chinese buyers particularly shun number 424: "die and die again."

*David Lung, "Heaven, Earth and Man (Master's thesis, University of Oregon, 1978).

Appendix 4

CHINESE ASTROLOGY

Doing the right thing, whether it is moving into a house or office, having a funeral, or marrying, at the right time is crucial to the Chinese. Some executives will not hold press conferences, break ground for buildings, or travel abroad unless the moment is propitious. To determine the correct day and hour for an event, Chinese throughout Asia either consult a feng shui man or fortune-teller or peruse an almanac offering not only assessments of the future but also helpful hints on subjects ranging from farming to face-reading. Feng shui men and fortune-tellers can charge from a couple of dollars for good travel days to hundreds for a ground-breaking date. Chinese more often do it themselves, seeking the aid of the almanac. One Chinese-American employee at the State Department said his wife consults the almanac on when to make a bid for a house or when to sell their car. "It's amazing," he comments. "Things always work to our advantage."

This all ties in, of course, with Chinese astrology. Marriages were once arranged according to complementary birthdays. Still, today, some Chinese pay attention to the astrological congeniality of their partners. Unlike Western astrology, which stresses months, the Chinese method is based on the twelve animal years of the Chinese lunar calendar. Each year represents an animal that bestows certain general character traits on those born in that time span.

The Rat (1900, 1912, 1924, 1936, 1948, 1960, 1972, 1984) possesses attributes ranging from charming and humorous to honest and meticulous. The Chinese say those born in these years make good and wise advisers, yet they can never decide for themselves, and change directions constantly. However, rats at times hunger for power and money, leading some to be gamblers, others to be manipulative or petty. Their greed can lead them into a destructive trap.

The Ox (1901, 1913, 1925, 1937, 1949, 1961, 1973, 1985) works hard, patiently, and methodically. These people enjoy helping others. Behind this tenacious, laboring, and self-sacrificing exterior lies an active mind. While their balance and strength inspire confidence, oxen can seem rigid, stubborn, and slow. They must labor long hours to accomplish little. The Chinese say the time of year and day an ox is born is important in determining life-style. One woman in Hong Kong bragged that she would always be financially provided for with minimal effort on her part because she was born on a winter night. Oxen have little to do during the winter months, she explained, because the sweat of summer and fall harvesting is over and it is up to the farmer to feed and keep the oxen warm so they'll have strength for spring planting. Oxen born during agricultural months, however, are sentenced to a life of hard labor.

The Tiger (1901, 1914, 1926, 1938, 1950, 1962, 1974, 1986) is courageous, active, and self-assured and makes an excellent leader and protector; tigers attract followers and admirers. However liberal-minded tigers may be, they are passionate, rash, and resist the authority of others. Chinese say tigers born at night will be particularly restless, for night is the time they scavenge for food. The Western term for a particularly fierce woman is "dragon lady," but the Chinese call her an "old tiger lady." And for this reason some Chinese avoid having children in the Tiger Year—for fear of having a daughter.

The Rabbit (1903, 1915, 1927, 1939, 1951, 1963, 1975, 1987) is quick, clever, and ambitious, but seldom finishes what he starts. The rabbit is a social creature, tactful, cool, and sensitive to others. Yet, this calm can become aloof; the sensitivity can be quirky and thin-skinned; and the intelligence can become dilettantish. The rabbit is lucky: With brains and only a little hard labor, the rabbit can go far.

The Dragon (1904, 1916, 1928, 1940, 1952, 1964, 1976, 1988), to the Chinese, is born in the most desirable year. The imperial family adopted the all-powerful dragon symbol as its royal insignia. Possessing magical powers, the versatile dragon is capable of soaring to the highest heavenly heights or diving to the depths of the sea. On one hand shrewd, healthy, and full of vitality, the dragon also possesses a mystical side, intuitive, artistic, and strangely lucky. Dragons, however, can plunge pretty low, becoming irritable, stubborn, and impetuous. The dragon's mystical allure may become a bit too other-worldly, making him/her difficult to get close to. The dragon's unsatisfactory love life leads to a string of loves and marriages.

The Snake (1905, 1917, 1929, 1941, 1953, 1965, 1977, 1989) in Asia prefers to call himself "little dragon," indicating this, too, is a lucky year. Snakes are wise, philosophical, calm, and understanding. They are receptive and physically alluring, often fickle. Success and fame come easily to snakes. If crossed, they spit venom and can be selfish. They can be lazy and self-indulgent. Their innate elegance can at times be ostentatious.

The Horse (1906, 1918, 1930, 1942, 1954, 1966, 1978, 1990), charming and cheerful, is an extremely likable character. Hard-working, self-possessed, and sharp, the horse skillfully acquires power, wealth, and respect. However, the horse's sometimes appreciated frankness can be tactless. The horse's impatient pursuit of success may become selfish and predatory. Horses can be obstinate.

The Ram (1907, 1919, 1931, 1943, 1955, 1967, 1979, 1991), endowed with innate intelligence and artistic talent, will fare well in business. These people are good-natured and altruistic. However, their successes are limited to money; in family matters they will flounder. They can be a bit too wishy-washy, undisciplined, and irresponsible, and at times show a morose, misanthropic side.

The Monkey (1908, 1920, 1932, 1944, 1956, 1968, 1980, 1992) is lively, likable, and witty. Inventive and intelligent, those born in these years can solve most problems quickly and skillfully and are able to accomplish much in business. Often, however, monkeys are too clever for their own good and can be mettlesome, opportunistic, and unscrupulous to the point of being tricky and manipulative. They tend to be lazy, concentrating on small matters while ignoring more important issues.

The Cock (1909, 1921, 1933, 1945, 1957, 1969, 1981, 1993), hardworking, resourceful, and talented, is a self-assured person. Unlike our Western stereotype of chickens, the Chinese cock is courageous. In groups, they are vivacious, amusing, and popular. But cocks can be a bit too cocksure—strutting their stuff brazenly can be particularly annoying to relatives and close friends.

The Dog (1910, 1922, 1934, 1946, 1958, 1970, 1982, 1994) makes a faithful, honest, and courageous friend, has a deep sense of justice, and inspires confidence. These people tend to be both magnanimous and prosperous, yet they can also be dogged, guarded, and defensive. They accomplish goals quickly. But the dog never really relaxes. Despite appearing calm and at rest, his heart and mind are always jumping.

The Pig (1911, 1923, 1935, 1947, 1959, 1971, 1983, 1995) is sensitive, caring, and indulgent. Not only intelligent and cultured, the pigs also have a streak of bawdiness and earthiness. Their various indulgences can verge on gluttony. Unlike the conniving Machiavellian pigs of *Animal Farm,* Chinese pigs tend to be helpless and insecure. During fat spells they suddenly lose all and are unable to defend themselves, much less attack others. Pigs in general are lucky but lazy.

The Chinese have charted approximate marital compatibility:

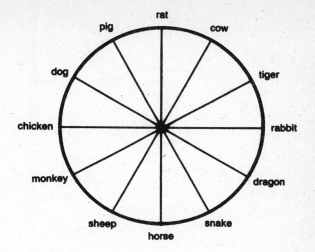

Bad marriages.

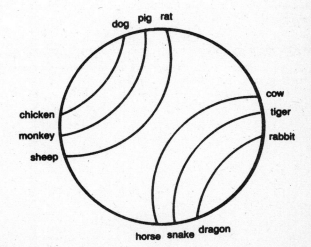

Chinese also avoid marriages between animals three years apart, except for Pig-Tiger and Snake-Monkey.

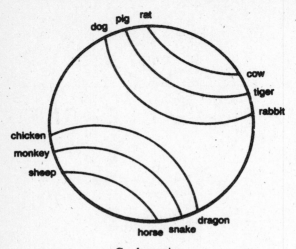

Good marriages.

Chinese astrology is in practice much more exacting than these generalities. In fact, one British woman married to a Chinese joked she had cesareans so her children would be born at an auspicious moment, thus pleasing her feng shui–conscious mother-in-law.

Appendix 5

THE FIVE ELEMENTS

The Chinese hope to improve their ch'i and fate by examining their five elements. Out of the interplay of yin and yang come five manifestations of ch'i: wood, earth, fire, water, and metal. Like yin and yang and ch'i, the five elements are not physical substances but powers or essences describing all matter and attributes. The Chinese associate these elements with time, space, matter, senses, colors, and psychological moods. For example, they assigned the element wood to spring, the color green, and the East. Fire heralded summer, the South, and red. Earth, positioned at the center, was mid-autumn and yellow. Metal is autumn, white, and the West. While water governs black (the deeper the water, the blacker it gets), the North, and winter.

The five elements have relative effects on each other, creating and destroying one another in a fixed succession. The cycle of development goes like this: Fire produces earth (ash); earth produces metal (minerals); metal creates water (although water rusts metal, this order derives from the observation that when water is in a metal cup, water forms on the outside of the vessel); water feeds wood (trees need water to grow); and wood aids fire. The chain of destruction is: wood harms earth; earth obstructs water; water destroys fire; fire melts metal; metal chops down wood.

Human ch'i can be divided into wood, earth, metal, water, and fire. Lin Yun says each person's nature possesses varying quantities of these corresponding natural elements. Each of the five human elements, he says, can be divided into seventy-two different types or amounts.

> Everyone has the five elements.* If someone is deficient in an element, this isn't necessarily bad. You first must check out the other elements to see whether they are well balanced. The ideal situation is to follow the mean, not have too much or too little of an element. On a scale of 1 to 72, the average 36 is the middle road, the most harmonious of natures. But if you have a lot or a little of an element, neither has a good or bad connotation, you simply must see all the elements in relation to each other.

The element wood, for example, stands for the Confucian ideal of benevolence, loyalty, and forgiveness. If a person possesses only a little wood, he is like a green leaf floating on a lake. When the east wind blows, he goes this way, when the west wind blows he goes that way: He is easily influenced. So whatever he hears, he agrees with or repeats. He doesn't have his own opinion.

A person with type-36 wood is like a growing tree: Under the influence of the wind his leaves flutter—meaning in the small things he is flexible—he bends but still has roots. When others say something, he listens, ponders all sides, and then makes his own decision. If he has a great deal of wood, he is like an old sturdy tree. When the wind blows, he isn't swept along. He doesn't listen to others (only to himself). He can be so inflexible that under a strong typhoon gust, he might break. He is prejudiced and just plain can't learn from others. No matter how long people talk to him, he still holds to his set position.

Metal, also translated as gold, stands for righteousness. People with little metal seldom speak, are very meticulous and careful, appear aloof and

---

*Traditional Chinese belief has it that males possess combinations of all five elements but that women should always be minus one element. If a woman has all five elements, she will not bear sons.

arrogant, strange and isolated. Little metal can also be the essence of a very independent person. A person possessing the mean of metal is fair, speaks the right amount, and always says the correct, appropriate thing. If someone is wrong he will criticize, but not overdo. In contrast, the person with a lot of metal tends to be unfair and self-righteous, leaping on any chance to gossip, criticize, and put his nose into others' business. He is argumentative and prone to complain. On the other hand, he can fight for principles and help and care for others. In Hong Kong, when a very talkative woman stopped her marathon monologue to ask Lin Yun about her five elements, he replied with a puckish grin, "Ah, you have an inordinate amount of gold/metal." This pleased her sense of self-righteousness and amused the bored and annoyed initiated who had listened to the soliloquy.

Fire is the element of wisdom, reason, and etiquette. When angered (literally "produce ch'i"), the person possessing little fire swallows his pride (ch'i) without expressing himself. When he is criticized, he doesn't speak up and ask for proof or defend himself. He is meek, with little passion to expend except for self-pity. The 36-person's anger is based on principle and logic. He knows how and when to put his foot down, but after he finishes stating his point or criticizing, he stops. The person with a maximum amount of fire can flare up without reason. He can be loud, unreasonable, unheeding, and highly critical of others.

A person short on earth, the element assigned to honesty and faith, will be an opportunist and a cheapskate. He'll easily scan a given situation and use it to his advantage. He has an eye out for good opportunities. He can be narcissistic, selfish, and slick. He may be a procrastinator and a cheater, always looking for shortcuts. People with a medium amount of earth are honest and dependable, very frank, and helpful to others. People who have lots of earth are like our aggy or hick. They are backward, old-fashioned, and unfashionable. Although something might be done to improve a situation or help themselves, they are scared to venture because people might criticize them, so they maintain their old customs. They do, however, like to help others to the point of self-sacrifice.

Lin Yun explains:

> If three friends, one with little earth, one with a medium amount, and another with lots of earth, go to a restaurant, the first two have $10 each, while the last has only $5. When the bill comes, the one with little earth will say he has only $5, the next will offer to lend the difference, and the third will offer to treat them all, though he's short on cash.

Lin Yun divides water—the element of insight, motivation, and social contacts—into living (or flowing) and dead (or still). Each person possesses both kinds. Flowing water is a person's drive and effectiveness in society. Still water reflects a person's clearness of mind. Lin Yun identifies seven of the seventy-two possible types of flowing water.

Of the moving variety, the smallest amount is valley water, which trickles down from a small mountain and then disappears (evaporates or seeps into a cave or a crack) before reaching level ground. These people are agoraphobic—they don't like to go out and are uneasy in open spaces. They prefer to spend time in the country and around the familiar sights of home. They also have a hard time mixing in society.

The second type of moving water is the fountain springing out of the ground, appearing glamorous, strong, and controlled, but in fact fountain water rises only to return to its pool and rise again. These people run around, expend a lot of energy, but get nowhere. Habitually, they go to the office, work, and return home. Lin Yun characterized a vivacious former actress as being a fountain. Every day she energetically performed chores for her family, entertained her husband's business associates and friends, and ended the day feeling tired and dissatisfied, only to replay her routine the next day.

The next is the stream whose activity is wider and whose progress may be meandering but ultimately has direction. When faced with an obstacle the stream may be set back for a brief interval, but it always finds a way to get around it and continue its course.

The rivers (the mean) are still more powerful and directed. They enjoy wider and unhindered social contacts and activity—seeing and making friends during vacation.

The large river has a lot of drive, but can flood over its shores or drag things along in its path, sometimes leaving chaos behind without being affected by it. He always accomplishes tasks efficiently. This is the prototype aggressive person.

The sea has a network of connections everywhere and travels a lot, touching people in different countries and different walks of life. It is the way of the jet-setter, or a social and political creature.

The ocean, although it has high and low tides, belongs on any shore. He is unpredictable, going in every direction, but attractive—all rivers flow to him.

The first type of the seventy-two varieties of still water, Lin Yun says, is the well water with limited vision and no movement in thought—a stagnant mind. The second type is sewer water—a person with unclear thoughts who clings to the wrong opinions and who is polluted from outside sources. The third type is troubled water, an unstable, hysterical person's assessment of things. The fourth type is muddy water, or someone with innate understanding who is nevertheless inarticulate and unclear. Pool water, on the other hand, has a clear knowledge that is learned and not instinctive. A person with pond water may have a clear understanding at home, but when he enters society his thought may be polluted by nearby roads (ideas), causing misunderstanding and poor decisions. Lake water stands for pure knowledge. As the sun and the moon rise and set, the middle of the lake shows the reflections. As things happen, the person reflects them like a mirror. He clearly knows what is going on and can intuit the essence of people and things around him.

Lin Yun's Tantric mysticism offers solutions to regulating and developing the five elements. Because the five elements are in fact five different manifestations of ch'i, the solutions are exercises and symbols to let ch'i adjust itself into the most balanced distribution. The exercises are the same for both quantities of too much or too little of an element. Lin Yun's solutions are not necessarily the most logical (for these cures to work, he says, they must be orally transmitted after the feng shui man is presented with a red ceremonial envelope). When people with too much metal are too talkative, logically we'd tell them to speak less. But Lin Yun maintains that this method is only cosmetic. For the best result the talkative should use breathing exercises. "This is a mouth problem," he says. "So you breathe through the mouth. In the morning when you get up, first inhale—but don't let out—one deep breath, then exhale it in nine short blows. The last breath should be the longest. Do this nine times for nine days or twenty-seven days if necessary."

For too much or too little wood, Lin Yun prescribes that, every morning right after arising, give the bed three or four shakes. Do this for nine days.

For an imbalance of earth, find a mole on the body nearest the heart. Then for nine days, on getting up, rub a cosmetic moisturizer on the mole, massaging in circular strokes the same number of years as your age.

To balance fire, carry something soft on the body—Lin Yun suggests suede, silk, or jade—jade's texture is cool and soft. Wear the object until your next birthday.

To balance water, Lin Yun prescribes a sort of chain-letter approach to control or further one's personal network of friends, one's activeness, and the amount of social contacts and judgment. For nine or twenty-seven days, you should meet or contact, by writing, calling, or seeing, nine new friends.

Traditional Chinese practice is more literal. In Hong Kong, a rich and intelligent man discovered when consulting a fortune-teller/feng shui expert during a business lull that he was short of fire. To correct this, he arranged in his entrance parlor an altar with an image of a fire god lit by a red electric light bulb. Supposedly, to the day he died he kept it lit in his front hall and business was always good.

The other five elements' antidotes are even more graphic. One longtime Hong Kong resident explained:

If you're short of wood then buy a wooden door or bed. If you're short of water, put a fish bowl or water basin in your room and office. (Water is especially important for businessmen because water is slang for money.) If you're short on earth, then you must be closer to the ground, and not live on a top floor of a highrise. Pick a bungalow with foundations next to the earth and have a lot of flowerpots filled with earth and plants. If you're short on gold, well, that's easy, you wear gold next to you.

Everyone's ch'i reacts to a color. Not all colors, however, affect everybody the same way. Some colors enhance a person's aura and others detract.

To assess a person's best color, first analyze his ch'i to discern his strong element—earth, fire, water, metal, wood. All five elements represent colors: wood is blue/green, fire is red, earth is yellow/brown, metal is white, water is black. These colors follow the five element cycles of mutual growth and decay. Once the element is found, use the cycle of development to see which element's color will enhance it. For example, people with a lot of wood should wear black (the color of water), while white (the metal color) will generally be bad for luck. Someone with lots of water should wear white and avoid yellow (the earth color). This can also work for buildings and interior design. Lin Yun said the United States' luck might well improve if yellow flowers were planted around the White House.

BIBLIOGRAPHY

Ayscough, Florence. *A Chinese Mirror*. Boston: Houghton Mifflin, 1925.

Bleibtreu, John. *The Parable of the Beast*. New York: The Macmillan Company, 1968.

Boyd, Andrew. *Chinese Architecture and Town Planning 1500 B.C.–A.D. 1911*. Chicago: University of Chicago Press, 1962.

Burkhardt, V. R. *Chinese Creeds and Customs*. 3 vols. Hong Kong, n.d.

Capra, Fritjof. *The Tao of Physics*. New York: Bantam Books, 1977.

De Bary, Wm. Theodore, ed. *Sources of Chinese Tradition*. 3 vols. New York and London: Columbia University Press, 1970.

Edkins, Rev. Joseph. *Chinese Buddhism*. London, 1893. Reprint. New York: Paragon, 1968.

Eitel, Ernest. *Feng Shui: or the Rudiments of Natural Science in China*. Hong Kong, 1873.

Eliade, Mircea. *The Sacred and the Profane*. Translated by Willard R. Trask. New York: Harcourt, Brace, 1959.

Feng, Yu-lan. *A Short History of Chinese Philosophy*. Translated and edited by Derek Bodde. New York and London: The Macmillan Company, 1948.

———. *The Spirit of Chinese Philosophy*. Translated by E. R. Hughes. Boston: Beacon Press, 1967.

Feuchtwang, Stephan D. R. *An Anthropological Analysis of Chinese Geomancy*. Vientiane, Laos, 1974.

Frazer, James George. *The Golden Bough*. New York: The Macmillan Company, 1951.

Graham, David Crockett. *Folk Religion in Southwest China*. Washington, D.C.: Smithsonian Institution Press, 1961.

Hawkes, David. *A Little Primer of Tu Fu*. New York: Oxford University Press, 1967.

Hitching, Francis. *Earth Magic*. New York: William Morrow, 1977.

I Ching, or Book of Changes, The. 2 vols. Translated by Richard Wilhelm, rendered into English by Cary F. Baynes. Princeton, N.J.: Princeton University Press, 1950.

Keswick, Maggie. *The Chinese Garden*. New York: Rizzoli, 1978.

Korda, Michael. *Power!* New York: Random House, 1975.

Lee, Sherman. *Chinese Landscape Painting*. New York: Harper & Row, 1971.

Lip, Evelyn. *Chinese Geomancy*. Singapore, 1979.

Liu, Wu-chi, and Yucheng Lo, Irving. *Sunflower Splendor*. Bloomington, Ind.: University of Indiana Press, 1975.

Lung, David. *Heaven, Earth and Man*. Eugene, Oregon, 1978.

MacFarquhar, Roderick. *The Forbidden City: China's Ancient Capital*. New York: Newsweek, 1978.

Bibliography

MacKenzie, Donald. *Myths of China and Japan*. London: Gresham Publishing, 1939.

Meyer, Jeffrey I. *Peking as a Sacred City*. South Pasadena, Calif.: E. Langstaff, 1976.

Needham, Joseph. *The Shorter Science and Civilization in China*. 2 vols. Cambridge, Eng.: Cambridge University Press, 1980.

Plopper, C. H. *Chinese Religion Seen Through the Proverbs*. New York: Paragon, 1969.

Reischauer, Edwin O., and Fairbank, John K. *East Asia: The Great Tradition*. Boston: Houghton Mifflin, 1960.

Saso, Michael. *Taoism and the Rite of Cosmic Renewal*. Pullman, Wash.: Washington State University Press, 1972.

Sickman, Laurence, and Soper, Alexander. *The Art and Architecture of China*. New York: The Viking Press, 1978.

Sullivan, Michael. *Arts of China, The*. Rev. ed. Berkeley, Los Angeles, and London: University of California Press, 1979.

Village as Solar Ecology, The. East Falmouth, Mass.: The New Alchemy Institute, 1980.

Waley, Arthur. *The Analects*. New York: The Macmillan Company, 1938.

———. *The Book of Songs*. New York: Grove Press, 1978.

———. *Translations from the Chinese*. New York: Alfred A. Knopf, 1941.

———. *The Way and Its Power*. New York: The Macmillan Company, 1958.

Watson, Burton, trans. *Cold Mountain: 100 Poems by Han-Shan*. New York: Grove Press, 1962.

White, Suzanne. *Suzanne White's Book of Chinese Chance*. New York: M. Evans, 1978.

Woolf, Virginia. *A Room of One's Own*. New York and London: Harcourt, Brace & World, 1957.

Yang, C. K. *Religion in Chinese Society*. Berkeley and Los Angeles: University of California Press, 1967.

Yoon, Hong-key. *Geomantic Relationships Between Culture and Nature in Korea*. South Pasadena, Calif.: E. Langstaff, 1976.

ARKANA – TIMELESS WISDOM FOR TODAY

With over 150 titles currently in print, Arkana is the leading name in quality books for mind, body, and spirit. Arkana encompasses the spirituality of both East and West, ancient and new. A vast range of interests is covered, including Mythology, Psychology and Transformation, Health, Science and Mysticism, Women's Spirituality, Zen, Western Traditions, and Astrology.

If you would like a catalogue of Arkana books, please write to:

Sales Dept. — Arkana
Penguin USA
375 Hudson St.
New York, NY 10014

Arkana Marketing Department
Penguin Books Ltd.
27 Wrights Lane
London W8 5TZ